FAST & FANTASTIC

The cover photo is by Fred Bird, courtesy of Canadian Living Magazine.

Copyright © 1986 by North Shore Family Services Society
6th Printing, November 1991

Canadian Cataloguing in Publication Data
Main entry under title:
Fast & Fantastic

ISBN 0-9694116-0-X

1. Quick and easy cookery. I. North Shore Family Services Society. II. Title: Fast and Fantastic.
TX715.6.F38 1986   641.5'55   C90-421-5

Illustrator   Karol Doner
Design and Layout   Maria Baratta
Typeset by   Skume River Studios
Printed in Canada by D.W. Friesen & Son Ltd.

The Cookbook began as a fund raising project for North Shore Family Services Society of North and West Vancouver, British Columbia. This cookbook has been put together entirely by volunteers, and has been sold with spectacular success in Vancouver. By supporting this cookbook you have helped a non-profit organization to continue and expand its vital work in your community.

Thank you.

On behalf of the North Shore Family Services Society, board, staff and clients, we wish to extend thanks to the many individuals who so generously and enthusiastically contributed to the creation of this cookbook.

To the "chefs" who shared their treasures; to the cooks, who tested every recipe; to the artists, typists and proofreaders who developed them, congratulations.

Your creativity and dedication have resulted in a unique and valued product which by its very existence expresses your commitment to enhance the quality of family life on the North Shore.

Heartfelt thanks to our patient families who ate Caviar Pie and Vitello Tonnato when they craved hamburgers.

We also thank the following for their valuable assistance and advice:

Dorothy Brown
Arlene Gladstone
Pat Johnston
Susan Mendelson
Earl Schmidt
Diana Whyte

The Cookbook Committee:

Doreen Ramage, Chairman
Gail Marus
Beth McAdams
Nancy Thordarson
John Calder
Gary Grafton
Mary Falconer
Roy Nelson

Our recipe contributors:

Joan Akers
Ann Ashcroft
Di Bailey
Marty Barregar
Joan Barter
Angela Bell
Joyce Birch
Jeanette Bourbonnais
Peggy Bridge
Ann Brodeur
Bobby Brodeur
Dorothy Brown
Lois Clarke
Eleanor Cordingley
Ginny Crawford
Nick Davies
Donna Dawson
Diane Dean
Jean Denault
Anne Dobell
Joanne Ellis
Geri Falloon
Phyllis Faulkner
Jill Flemons
Annabelle Gaffney
Nancy Gallop
Lorna Gladney
Arlene Gladstone
Judy Gosney
Jean Gowdey
Marg Greaves
Brenda Greenberg
Sigrun Hanna
Sandy Haras
Bev Hargraft
Sylvia Hassan
Adrienne Hebert
Freida Henderson
Diane Hogan
Isabelle Howells
Arlene Hudson
Nina Huumo

Penny Jacob
Jacqueline James
Pat Johnston
Audrey Johnstone
Jean Jones
Pat Kayll
Muriel Kerr
Anne LaFleur
Judy Langstaff
Nancy Lavorato
Sue Laxton
Marg Lemoine
Lucille Lewis
Little Gun Lake Lodge
May Loudon
Anna Luckyj
Heather McAdams
Hugh McAdams
Grace McAdams
Ann McBride
Barbara McBride
Judy McGladdery
Judy McKay
Barbara MacDougall
Mimi MacKinnon
Gay McLenaghon
Wendy McSorley
Lois Martin
Emily Merino
Terry Mills
Monique Molleur
Louise Monkman
Anne Morison
Tazeem Nathoo
Charlotte Nelson
Joyce Neufeld
Betty Jane Norris
Jennifer Park
Marguerite Patterson
Lola Pawer
Peggy Pedersen
Marilyn Ployart

Our recipe contributors: cont.

Cathy Ramage
Myrtle Ramage
Joan Rayson
Mark Rayter
Elise Rees
Richard Rees
Barbara Reid
Bonnie Robertson
Elizabeth Robinson
Brenda Robson
Marlene Rockliff
Judy Rogstad
Marilyn Ross
Jayne Russcken
Diane Rutledge
Cora Ryan
Jayne St. John
Sherrill Samis
Alison Solven
Sandy Sport
Angie Snyder
Nancy Stewart
Jean Taylor
Dana Thordarson
Marg Waddell
Claudia Webber
Leigh Webber
Sharon Westin
Sandy Whitfield
Diana Whyte
Joan Walker
Sharon Woyat

Table of Contents

Hors d'oeuvres 1

Starters 17

Soups 29

Salads 45

Entrées 59

Vegetables 87

Casual 103

Breads 123

Desserts 139

Cookies & Squares 161

Et Cetera 173

Index 177

Hors D'Oeuvres

Cream Cheese and Crab Delight

Fresh shrimp may be substituted for the crab in this recipe.

8	oz	cream cheese	250 g
1	Tbsp	Worcestershire sauce	15 mL
1	Tbsp	lemon juice	15 mL
1	Tbsp	minced onion	15 mL
1	Tbsp	minced parsley	15 mL
½	tsp	dried dill	2 mL
⅛	tsp	garlic powder	.5 mL
⅔	cup	chili sauce or seafood sauce	150 mL
½	lb	crabmeat	250 g
		parsley for garnish	

Blend together the first 7 ingredients. Spread in a 7" (17 cm) circle on a serving plate. Cover with chili sauce and top with crab. Garnish with additional parsley. May be covered and refrigerated up to 24 hours. Serve with crackers or thin rounds of crusty bread.
Serves 10 - 12.

Antipasto

A can-opener special - ready in a jif!

2		cans (6½oz/184g) solid pack tuna, including oil	2
1		can (10oz/284g) mushroom stems and pieces, drained	1
½		jar (16oz/500mL) sweet mixed pickles with onions and cauliflower, drained and chopped	½
2		small carrots, thinly sliced	2
2-3		stalks celery, chopped	2-3
⅔	cup	ketchup	150 mL
⅔	cup	chili sauce	150 mL
1		can (10oz/294g) french cut green beans	1

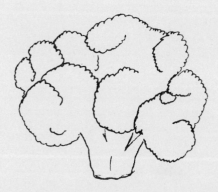

Flake tuna in a large bowl. Add remaining ingredients mixing well. Add green beans last so they don't break up too much. Put in containers and store in the refrigerator up to 5 weeks.
Makes about 2qt (2L).

Mock Pâté Aspic

Makes expensive pâté go a long way!

1		envelope unflavored gelatin	1
¼	cup	water	50 mL
1		can (10oz/284mL) consommé	1
1		can (14oz/400g) Pâté de Fois Gras	1
		salt and pepper	
		tarragon	
		parsley	

Put gelatin and water in saucepan; heat; stir until gelatin is dissolved. Heat soup; blend in pâté. Add gelatin and seasonings. Pour into oiled mold. Refrigerate until set. Serve as a spread or sliced on a lettuce leaf with melba toast and cucumber rounds on the side. This recipe may be prepared a day or two in advance.
Serves many as hors d'oeuvres or 8 as a starter.

Hot Artichoke Hearts

1		can (14oz/398mL) artichoke hearts	1
½	cup	grated parmesan cheese	125 mL
1	cup	mayonnaise	250 mL
½	tsp	garlic salt	2 mL
1	tsp	lemon juice	5 mL

Preheat oven to 350°F (180°C). Drain and chop artichokes. Mix with remaining ingredients. Place in a 1qt (1L) casserole.
Bake for 10 minutes. Serve hot with crackers.
Serves 6 - 8

Greek Spinach Rolls

10	oz	spinach, cooked, drained and chopped	300	g
1		onion, chopped	1	
3		green onions, chopped	3	
3	Tbsp	olive oil	45	mL
3		eggs	3	
½	lb	feta cheese	250	g
¾	cup	cottage cheese	175	mL
¼	cup	breadcrumbs	50	mL
½	tsp	salt	2	mL
¼	tsp	pepper	1	mL
¾	lb	filo pastry leaves	350	g
¼	lb	butter, melted	125	g

Preheat oven to 425°F (220°C). Sauté onions in oil until soft. Add spinach. Combine the next 6 ingredients and add to spinach mixture. Set aside. Working quickly, brush each layer of filo with melted butter. Stack six leaves on top of each other. Repeat. Divide spinach along the long edge of the 6 layers. Seal by folding sides toward centre and then roll up like a jelly roll. Repeat for second roll. Place on greased baking sheet. Brush outside with melted butter.
Caution: Keep the pastry sheets that you are not working with, covered with waxed paper or plastic wrap as filo dries out very quickly.
Bake 20 minutes. Cut in slices to serve.
Makes 8 slices per roll.

Shrimp in Jellied Consommé

Always a hit because they're unique!

¾	cup	medium size shrimp	175	mL
1		can (10oz/284mL) consommé	1	
1		envelope (1oz/28g) unflavored gelatin	1	
		Worcestershire sauce to taste		
		melba toast rounds or other round crackers		
		mayonnaise		

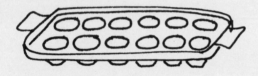

Use plastic egg containers or small muffin pans. Recipe makes at least 36 at once. Heat soup, gelatin, and Worcestershire sauce in saucepan until gelatin is dissolved. Place 1 shrimp in each hole in tray. Cover with soup mixture. Refrigerate until firm. Loosen edges with knife (a curved grapefruit knife works well) and turn out on crackers; spread with mayonnaise. Jellied rounds may be made days ahead. Store in layers separated with plastic wrap.

Note: This recipe is also excellent as a first course. Place 4-6 shrimp in the bottom of a regular muffin tin. Turn out onto lettuce leaves and serve as jellied salad.

Makes 36 hors d'oeuvres.

Howe Sound Crab Mousse

In a word - wonderful!

1		can (10oz/284mL) cream of mushroom soup	1
8	oz	cream cheese	250 g
1		envelope unflavored gelatin	1
¼	cup	cold water	50 mL
½	cup	finely chopped celery	125 mL
½	cup	finely chopped green onions	125 mL
1	cup	mayonnaise	250 mL
½-¾	lb	crabmeat	250-350 g
¼	tsp	curry powder	1 mL

Heat together soup and cream cheese stirring until smooth. Add gelatin to cold water and soften 5 minutes. Add to soup mixture and stir to dissolve. Add remaining ingredients. Mix well. Pour into a 4 cup (1L) mold and chill overnight. Unmold, garnish and serve with crackers. Serves a crowd.

Onion Rounds

Après ski favorites!

1		baguette	1
¼	cup	butter or margarine	50 mL
¼	cup	finely chopped onion	50 mL
1	cup	mayonnaise	250 mL
½	tsp	curry powder	2 mL

Slice bread thinly and butter each slice. Mix remaining ingredients and spread on slices of bread. Place slices on cookie sheet and broil until bubbly and tinged brown. Serve hot.
Serves the ski team!

Salmon Party Log

Surround with your favorite crackers or cocktail bread and watch it disappear!

2		cans (7¾oz/220g) red sockeye salmon	2
8	oz	cream cheese, softened	250 g
1	Tbsp	lemon juice	15 mL
1	tsp	prepared horseradish	5 mL
1	Tbsp	green onions, snipped	15 mL
¼	tsp	salt	1 mL
½	cup	pecans, chopped	125 mL
3	Tbsp	fresh parsley, snipped	45 mL

Drain salmon, remove skin and bones, then flake. Combine the next 5 ingredients. Add salmon and mix thoroughly. Chill several hours or overnight. Combine pecans and parsley. Shape salmon mixture into a 8" (20cm) log, roll in nut mixture, and chill well.
Serves 12.

Tuna Teasers

1	cup	flour	250 mL
1½	tsp	baking powder	7 mL
1	tsp	onion salt	5 mL
½	tsp	curry powder	2 mL
		dash of cayenne pepper	
¼	cup	butter	50 mL
½	cup	milk	125 mL
1		can (6½oz/184 g) flaked tuna fish, drained	1
1	cup	shredded cheddar cheese	250 mL
1	Tbsp	finely minced green pepper	15 mL

Preheat oven to 450°F (230°C). Combine first 5 ingredients. Cut in butter until mixture resembles fine crumbs. Add milk and stir until blended. Add last 3 ingredients. Mix well. Drop by teaspoonfuls onto lightly greased baking sheet.
Bake for 10-12 minutes until golden brown.
Note: Also good served with soup or tomato juice
Makes 36 small puffs.

Gouda Squares

Easy and wonderful!

| 8 | oz | stick of gouda cheese | 250 g |
| 8 | oz | pkg refrigerated crescent rolls | 235 g |

Preheat oven to 375°F (190°C). Cut cheese into three lengthwise slices. Unroll 4 crescent rolls on baking sheet and press perforations together to form a rectangle. Place cheese slices on top. Unroll remaining 4 rolls, pressing perforations together. Place on top of cheese. Press outside edges together to seal.
Bake for 17 minutes. Cut in squares.
Serves 6 - 8

Clam Puffs

1	cup	cream cheese	250 mL
1		can (10oz/284mL) baby clams, drained and minced	1
1	Tbsp	sherry	15 mL
1	tsp	Worcestershire sauce	5 mL
¼	cup	onion, finely chopped	50 mL
		toast rounds, water crackers, or thin slices of baguette bread	

Combine ingredients and spread on toast rounds, crackers or bread. Broil mid oven until golden and puffy.
Makes about 24 - 2" (5cm) rounds.

Mary's Gravlax

Swedish marinated salmon.

2		salmon fillets (approx 4-5lbs (2-2.5kg)	2
1		bunch fresh dill	1
¼	cup	coarse salt	50 mL
¼	cup	sugar	50 mL
2	Tbsp	crushed peppercorns	30 mL
1	tsp	white vinegar	5 mL

Place 1 fillet, skin side down, in a deep non-metal container. Wash dill and shake dry; place on top of fish. Combine next 3 ingredients; sprinkle evenly over dill. Moisten with vinegar. Top with second fillet, skin side up. Cover with foil and place weight on top. Refrigerate 2 or 3 days, turning fish every 12 hours; basting with liquid marinade that accumulates. When done, remove fish from marinade, rinse away seasonings and pat dry. Place the separated halves, skin side down, and slice thinly on the diagonal. Serve with toast or thin black bread, lemon wedges, freshly ground pepper and mustard sauce.

Mustard Sauce

¼	cup	Dijon mustard	50 mL
1	tsp	dry mustard	5 mL
3	Tbsp	chopped fresh dill	45 mL
3	Tbsp	sugar	45 mL
2	Tbsp	white vinegar	30 mL
⅓	cup	vegetable oil	75 mL

Blend first 5 ingredients in food processor using steel knife. Slowly pour in oil and blend until it forms a thick mayonnaise.

Chicken Wings

2	lbs	chicken wings, tips removed and each wing cut in half	1 kg

The following sauces give variety to this popular "make ahead" appetizer. Serves 8.

Zippy!

¼	cup	soy sauce	50 mL
¼	cup	vegetable oil	50 mL
½	tsp	Worcestershire sauce	2 mL
⅓	cup	brown sugar	75 mL
½	tsp	ground ginger	2 mL
½	tsp	cayenne pepper	2 mL
½	tsp	chili peppers	2 mL
½	tsp	paprika	2 mL
3		garlic cloves, crushed	3

Combine ingredients in large shallow bowl. Add wings and turn to coat. Refrigerate at least 2 hours, turning once during this time. Spread wings on rack in baking pan. Brush with remaining soy sauce mixture.
Bake at 425°F (220°C) for 25 minutes, until golden, turning half way through and brushing with marinade.

Saucy!

½	cup	brown sugar	125 mL
¼	cup	melted butter	50 mL
¼	cup	chili sauce	50 mL
½	cup	ketchup	125 mL
2	Tbsp	white vinegar	30 mL
¼	tsp	chili powder	1 mL
3	Tbsp	Worcestershire sauce	45 mL
3	Tbsp	prepared mustard	45 mL

Combine ingredients in shallow bowl. Dip wings in sauce and place on rack in baking pan.
Bake at 425°F (220°C) for 25 minutes, turning halfway through and brushing again with sauce.
Serve with leftover sauce.
Makes about 2 dozen.

Lemon-y!

¼	cup	lemon juice	50 mL
¼	cup	soy sauce	50 mL
3	Tbsp	honey	45 mL
3	Tbsp	minced fresh ginger root	2 mL
		or	
½	tsp	ground ginger	2 mL
¼	cup	water	50
2	Tbsp	finely chopped onion	30 mL

Combine ingredients in large bowl. Place wings in sauce and marinate for 2 hours. Place wings on rack in pan.
Bake at 425°F (220°C) for 25 minutes. Turn halfway through baking and baste with additional marinade.

Buon Gusto!

½	cup	butter	125 mL
1		garlic clove, peeled and halved	1
¾	cup	flour	175 mL
⅓	cup	grated parmesan cheese	75 mL
½	tsp	dried oregano	2 mL
½	tsp	dried thyme	2 mL
1	tsp	salt	5 mL
¼	tsp	pepper	1 mL

Preheat oven to 400°F (200°C). Butter 9x12" (23x30cm) pan. Sauté garlic in ½ cup (125mL) butter for 5 minutes. Discard garlic. Combine next 6 ingredients in a plastic bag. Add chicken wings separately; shake to coat. Roll in garlic butter, one at a time, and place close together in baking pan.
Bake 30 minutes. Turn chicken and continue baking 25 minutes or until brown and tender.

Mexican Flour Tortilla Rolls

Make 2 days before serving.

3		pkg (8oz/250g) cream cheese, softened	3	
1	cup	sour cream	250	mL
1	Tbsp	Picante Sauce (medium)	15	mL
10		green onions, chopped	10	
		juice of 1 lime		
1		jalapeno pepper, seeded and chopped	1	
1-2		pkg floured tortillas	1-2	
		Picante Sauce		

Two days before serving, mix all ingredients together, spread on tortillas, and roll up. Store in layers, covering each layer with a damp paper towel followed by plastic wrap. Refrigerate. On day of serving cut rolls into 1" (2.5cm) slices and place around a centre bowl filled with Picante sauce. Dip in sauce.
Serves many.

Quick'n'Easy Sausage Cheese Balls

1	lb	sausage meat	500	g
1	lb	grated sharp cheddar cheese	500	g
3	cups	packaged biscuit mix	750	mL

Preheat oven to 350°F (180°C). Combine all ingredients.
Form into balls and bake for 15 minutes. May be frozen on a cookie sheet and stored in bags ready to use. Serve on toothpicks and dip in plum sauce.

Plum Sauce

1		jar (12oz/350mL) plum jam	1	
2	Tbsp	vinegar	30	mL
1	Tbsp	brown sugar	15	mL
1	Tbsp	finely chopped onion	15	mL
1	tsp	crushed red pepper	5	mL
1		clove garlic, minced	1	
½	tsp	ground ginger	2	mL

Combine all ingredients in a saucepan. Bring to a boil, stirring constantly. Remove from heat; cool. Refrigerate, covered, overnight. Serve warm or cold. Also good with pork or fowl.
Makes 1¼ cups.
Feeds a crowd.

Chinese Sweet and Sour Meatballs

1½	lb	lean ground beef	750	g
1	tsp	salt	5	mL
½	tsp	pepper	2	mL

Batter

2		eggs, beaten	2	
¼	cup	flour	50	mL
1	tsp	salt	5	mL
1	cup	oil	250	mL

Sauce

3		green peppers, diced	3	
1		can (10oz/284mL) pineapple chunks, drained	1	
1	cup	beef broth	250	mL
3	Tbsp	cornstarch	45	mL
1	Tbsp	soy sauce	15	mL
½	cup	cider vinegar	125	mL
½	cup	sugar	125	mL

Shape first 3 ingredients into 24 balls. Mix batter. Dip meatballs in batter. Heat oil in frypan and brown meatballs over low heat. Remove. Pour off all but 2 Tbsp of oil. To this, add next 3 ingredients and cook over low heat 10 minutes. Mix next 4 ingredients and stir into mixture and cook until thickened. Return meatballs and cook over low heat 5 minutes. Serve.
These meatballs may be served from a chafing dish but are better if removed from sauce after cooking and passed on platter with toothpicks and additional sauce on side.
Makes 24 balls.

Starters

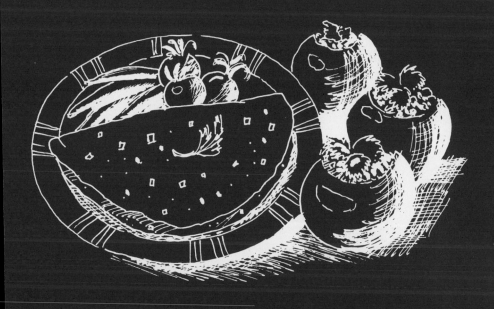

Fried Cheese Italian Style

1	lb	mozzarella cheese	500 g
3		beaten eggs	3
¼	cup	flour	50 mL
⅔	cup	breadcrumbs, seasoned or plain	150 mL
1		garlic clove, minced	1
1	Tbsp	cooking oil	15 mL
1		can(28oz/796mL) tomatoes, drained and chopped	1
¼	tsp	salt	1 mL
		pepper to taste	
1	tsp	dried oregano	5 mL
1	tsp	sugar	5 mL
¼	tsp	dried basil	1 mL
¼	cup	cooking oil	50 mL

Cut cheese into 2" x 2" x 1/2"(5 x 1 x 5cm) slices approximately. Dip in egg, then flour, then egg again, then in crumbs. Place on wax paper-lined baking sheet and refrigerate 1 hour. In saucepan, cook garlic in 1 Tbsp oil; add next 6 ingredients. Simmer uncovered 45 minutes. Set aside. In skillet, fry cheese in oil until brown, turning once (2½ -5 minutes altogether). Drain on paper towelling. Serve with sauce. Serves 4.

Smoked Salmon Mousse

Sinfully rich!

1	lb	smoked salmon	500	g
2	Tbsp	lemon juice	30	mL
¼	cup	unsalted butter, melted	50	mL
2	Tbsp	vodka or gin	30	mL
1	cup	whipping cream	250	mL
		salt and pepper		

In food processor, blend first 4 ingredients. With motor running, add cream through the feed tube. Blend in seasonings. Pour into mold and chill. May be frozen and defrosted before serving. Serve sliced or scooped on lettuce leaf with pumpernickel bread, melba rounds or cucumber slices on the side.
Makes approximately 3½ cups(875mL).

Caviar Pie

Caviar is an elegant start to any dinner.

1		large avocado	1	
3	Tbsp	finely chopped onion	45	mL
6		hardboiled eggs, chopped	6	
3	Tbsp	mayonnaise	45	mL
1		jar(3½oz/114mL) lumpfish caviar	1	

Mash avocado and spread in an 8"(20cm) pie plate. Sprinkle onion over avocado. Mix eggs and mayonnaise; spread over onions. Sprinkle caviar over all; chill. Serve cut in pie shaped wedges on lettuce leaf with crackers on the side.
Serves 8.

Terrine of Sole and Salmon

An elegant make ahead first course or luncheon dish.
Serve with Hollandaise sauce.

Sole Mousseline

½	lb	sole fillets cut in 1"(2½cm) pieces	250 g
1	Tbsp	slightly beaten egg white	15 mL
⅓	cup	cold heavy cream	75 mL
2	Tbsp	minced fresh parsley	30 mL
2	Tbsp	minced fresh chives	30 mL
⅛	tsp	salt	.5 mL
		pinch of white pepper	

Salmon Mousseline

½	lb	skinless salmon fillets cut in 1"(2½cm) pieces	250 g
1	Tbsp	slightly beaten egg white	15 mL
⅔	cup	cold heavy cream	150 mL
⅛	tsp	salt	.5 mL
		pinch of cayenne pepper	

Prepare a 1 quart(1L) rectangular terrine by buttering the inside and then lining with well buttered waxed paper that has been cut to fit smoothly.

Sole Mousseline
Combine ingredients in a food processor or blender and purée until smooth. Spoon into prepared terrine and smooth to level.

Salmon Mousseline
Preheat oven to 350°F (180°C). Prepare as for sole mousseline, spoon over sole layer and smooth top. Cover with buttered waxed paper and a double layer of foil, and place in a baking pan. Pour enough hot water into pan to reach half way up the sides of the terrine.
Bake for 50 minutes or until a knife inserted in the centre comes out clean. Remove foil and pour off any liquid. Cool. May be refrigerated at this point and served cold or reheated.
Serves 4.

Seafood Salad Bowls

¼	cup	chili sauce	50 mL
3	Tbsp	finely chopped onions	45 mL
3	Tbsp	finely chopped celery	45 mL
3	Tbsp	finely chopped green pepper	45 mL
½	tsp	salt	2 mL
2	tsp	horseradish	10 mL
½	cup	unflavored yogurt	125 mL
¼	cup	sour cream	50 mL
¼	cup	mayonnaise	50 mL
2	cups	flaked cooked fish or shellfish	500 mL

tomato shells
parsley sprigs or lemon twists for garnish

Halve tomatoes and scoop out pulp. Combine all other ingredients and place in tomato shells. Garnish with parsley sprigs or lemon twists and serve on lettuce leaves.
Serves 6-8.

Gratin de Coquille St. Jacques

½	cup	butter, softened	125 mL
1	cup	sliced mushrooms	250 mL
3	Tbsp	finely chopped green onions	45 mL
1	Tbsp	finely chopped garlic	15 mL
2	cups	scallops	500 mL
½	cup	breadcrumbs	125 mL
½	cup	chopped parsley	125 mL
		salt and pepper to taste	

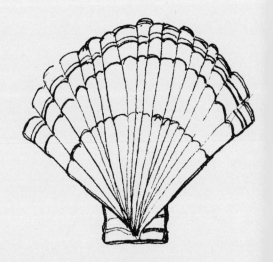

Preheat oven to 450°F (230°C). Melt ¼ cup (50mL) butter in skillet; add mushrooms; sauté until wilted. Add onions and garlic; cook for one minute. Pour into bowl; add 2 Tbsp (30mL) butter and the remaining ingredients. Fill 6 seafood shells with mixture. Put shells on baking sheet. Melt last 2 Tbsp (30mL) butter and drizzle over shells. Run shells under broiler until nicely browned on top. (1 - 2 min.) Serves 6.

Salmon Tartare with Black Caviar

1	lb	smoked salmon	500 g
2		hardboiled eggs, cut in quarters	2
1		thin onion slice	1
¼	tsp	freshly ground pepper	1 mL
		watercress or lettuce leaves	
8	tsp	black caviar	40 mL
8		lemon slices	8

Place first 4 ingredients in food processor. Blend until smooth. Spoon into mold(s) and refrigerate, covered. Unmold onto watercress or lettuce leaf. Top with caviar and serve with lemon slices on the side. Serves 8.

Mark's Fusili Shrimp Salad

May be prepared ahead of time and refrigerated. Allow to stand at room temperature for 2 hours before serving.

1	lb	cooked and cleaned shrimp	500	g
½	lb	tri-colored fusili	250	g
1		red pepper	1	
1		green pepper	1	
		salt, pepper to taste		
⅓	cup	white wine vinegar	75	mL
1	Tbsp	Dijon mustard	15	mL
1	tsp	dried basil	5	mL
⅔	cup	olive oil	150	mL
		salt, pepper to taste		
2	Tbsp	fresh parsley, chopped	30	mL

Cook fusili in salted, boiling water, 4-6 minutes after water returns to a boil (1 to 2 teaspoons of oil in the water prevents the pasta from sticking). Rinse and toss pasta in colander, using cold water. Season with salt and pepper. Char peppers over an open flame or under broiler until skins are blackened. Place peppers in plastic bag and steam over boiling water for 6 minutes. Peel charred skin from peppers, remove seeds, and cut into fusili length pieces. Mix vinegar, mustard and basil. Whisk in olive oil and salt and pepper to taste. Add peppers and shrimp. Combine with fusili. Sprinkle fresh parsley on top when serving.
Serves 8-10.

Special Avocado

A wonderful start to a dinner party.

4		avocados, unpeeled, pitted and cut in half lengthwise	4	
2	Tbsp	lemon juice	30	mL
8		slices crisp bacon, crumbled	8	
½	cup	butter	125	mL
¼	cup	brown sugar	50	mL
¼	cup	ketchup	50	mL
¼	cup	vinegar	50	mL
1	Tbsp	soy sauce	15	mL

Brush cut surface of avocado with lemon juice. Fill with bacon. Combine remaining ingredients and heat to boiling. Drizzle sauce over. Pass remaining sauce.
Serves 8.

Pasta Pronto!

Distinctive sauces to dress up your favorite pasta.

1		slice of bacon cut in small pieces	1
1	Tbsp	butter	15 mL
1		egg yolk	1
1	Tbsp	grated parmesan	15 mL
1	Tbsp	sour cream pepper	15 mL

Fry bacon until crisp. Drain. Toss cooked pasta with butter. Add bacon. Mix next 3 ingredients. Add to pasta and toss. Add pepper to taste. Serve immediately.
Serves 1.

Pasta Alle Vongole

2		garlic cloves, crushed	2
1	Tbsp	minced parsley	15 mL
1	Tbsp	oil	15 mL
1	Tbsp	butter	15 mL
1		can(14oz/398mL)tomatoes, crushed	1
1		can(10oz/284g)baby clams, drained salt, pepper and paprika to taste	1

Cook garlic and parsley in oil and butter for 2 - 3 minutes, stirring constantly so garlic does not stick. Add tomatoes and simmer 10 minutes. Add remaining ingredients and heat.
Enough sauce for 3 - 4 servings.

Pesto Pasta

2	cups	fresh well drained or dried basil leaves	500 mL
1	cup	grated parmesan cheese	250 mL
½	cup	olive oil	125 mL
4		cloves of garlic	4

Use metal blade of Cuisinart, mix all ingredients. Place in small jar, cover with thin layer of olive oil to prevent darkening, refrigerate up to a week or freeze for longer storage.
With pasta: to 4 cups (1000mL) fresh pasta, add 6 Tbsp (90mL) pesto sauce and 4 Tbsp (60mL) soft butter. Add 1 cup (250) parmesan cheese. Serve at once.

Feta-Mato Shrimp Sauce

¼	cup	olive or vegetable oil	50 mL
1		medium onion, finely chopped	1
½	cup	dry white wine	125 mL
1	Tbsp	finely chopped parsley	15 mL
4		medium tomatoes, coarsely chopped	4
½	tsp	oregano	2 mL
½	tsp	salt	2 mL
		black pepper to taste	
½	cup	crumbled feta cheese	125 mL
¾	lb	cooked, shelled shrimp	375 g
1	Tbsp	finely chopped parsley	15 mL

Heat oil in skillet and cook onions until soft. Add the next 6 ingredients. Bring to a boil and cook over high heat, uncovered until mixture thickens to a light purée. Stir in the cheese and shrimp and heat to warm through. Sprinkle with parsley. Serve over rice or pasta.
Serves 4.

Scallops Provençale and Avocado

16		green onions, chopped	16	
2		garlic cloves, finely minced	2	
2	tsp	dried basil	10	mL
1	tsp	dried tarragon	5	mL
¼	tsp	dried thyme	1	mL
3	Tbsp	butter	45	mL
3	Tbsp	vegetable oil	45	mL
½	cup	dry white wine	125	mL
1		can(28oz/796mL)crushed tomatoes	1	
½	cup	whipping cream	125	mL
2	tsp	sugar	10	mL
1	lb	sea scallops, quartered	500	g
1		large ripe avocado, chopped	1	

Sauté first 5 ingredients in the combined butter and oil. Add wine and cook 2 minutes more. Stir in tomatoes and boil briefly until sauce is thick. Add cream and sugar, stir. Add scallops to very hot sauce, do not boil. Pour sauce over pasta and toss. Serve, topped with avocado. Serves 4.

Soups

Bongo Bongo Soup

The pièce de résistance of any dinner party.

2	cups	milk	500 mL
½	cup	light cream	125 mL
8	oz	oysters, cooked and puréed	250 g
¾	cup	spinach, cooked and puréed	175 mL
2	tsp	butter	10 mL
1	tsp	Worcestershire sauce	5 mL
¼	tsp	salt	1 mL
¼	tsp	garlic powder	1 mL
		pepper to taste	
3	Tbsp	cold water	45 mL
1	Tbsp	cornstarch	15 mL
		parsley for garnish	

In a heavy saucepan heat together the first 9 ingredients. Mix the cornstarch and water and stir slowly into the soup mixture. Simmer and stir until thickened. Do not let the mixture boil. Serve in soup cups garnished with parsley.
Note: Make it a day ahead and reheat before serving.
Serves 6.

Scalloped Potato Soup

Don't be put off by the title. Try it; it's wonderful.

3		cans (10oz/284g) chicken broth	3
2½	cups	leftover scalloped potatoes	625 mL
2		zucchini, sliced	2
½	lb	fresh asparagus or peeled broccoli stalks	250 g
1	cup	cream	250 mL
		salt and pepper to taste	

Simmer the first 2 ingredients together for 20 minutes. Add the next 2 and simmer 20 minutes more. Purée in small batches in blender or food processor. Return to saucepan, add remaining ingredients. Heat and serve.
Serves 4-6.

Manhattan Clam Chowder

A pair of super chowders.

2		cans (10oz/284mL) baby clams	2	
5		slices bacon, chopped	5	
1		medium onion, chopped	1	
2	cups	chopped potatoes	500	mL
1	cup	chopped carrots	250	mL
1		stalk celery, chopped	1	
1		can (28oz/796mL) tomatoes, broken up	1	
½	tsp	salt	2	mL
¼	tsp	thyme	1	mL
¼	tsp	pepper	1	mL
1		bay leaf	1	

In a large heavy saucepan, sauté bacon and onion until bacon is cooked. Drain off fat. Add clam liquid, setting aside clams until later. Add remaining ingredients, cover and simmer 40 minutes. Add clams, heat and serve. Wonderful served with Mozzarella Loaf, and a crisp salad. Serves 6.

Boston Clam Chowder

¼	lb	butter	125	g
¼	lb	bacon, chopped	125	g
1½	cups	chopped celery	375	mL
1½	cups	chopped onions	375	mL
3		garlic cloves, minced	3	
½	cup	flour	125	mL
½	cup	cubed potatoes	125	mL
3		cans (10oz/284g) baby clams	3	
1		can (14oz/398mL) clam nectar	1	
4	cups	cream	1	L
1		bay leaf	1	
		white pepper to taste		

In a large heavy saucepan, cook the first 5 ingredients until the bacon is cooked. Add flour, stirring until thickened. Add remaining ingredients and simmer slowly for 45 minutes. Freezes well.
Serves 8.

Pacific Salmon Chowder

A super variation on the clam version.

1		can (15½oz/439g) salmon	1
2	cups	potatoes in cubes	500 mL
2	cups	boiling water	500 mL
1	cup	chopped onion	250 mL
1	cup	chopped celery	250 mL
1		can (19oz/540mL) tomatoes coarsely chopped	1
3	tsp	butter	15 mL
3	tsp	flour	15 mL
2	cups	milk	500 mL
		salt and pepper to taste	
		garnish with chopped parsley	

Remove skin and bones from salmon. Boil the water in a large saucepan and add the vegetables. Cover and simmer until the vegetables are tender. Add salmon and simmer for 5 to 10 minutes. In a second saucepan melt the butter, blend in the flour and slowly add milk. Cook and stir until smooth and thickened. Add white sauce to salmon mixture and heat gently - do not boil.
Serves 8.

Zucchini Soup

½	cup	chopped onion	125 mL
1		large garlic clove, crushed	1
3	Tbsp	butter	45 mL
6		medium zucchini, chopped	6
½	tsp	salt	2 mL
½	tsp	pepper	2 mL
6		chicken bouillon cubes	6
5	cups	boiling water	1250 mL
½	tsp	summer savory	2 mL
¼	tsp	thyme	1 mL
¼	tsp	tarragon	1 mL

Sauté the first 3 ingredients until the onion is soft. Add the next 3 ingredients. Cover and cook 10 minutes. Dissolve bouillon cubes in boiling water. Place the vegetables in a blender or food processor along with a little bouillon liquid. Blend until smooth. Return to saucepan along with remaining ingredients. Simmer 10 minutes.
Serves 8.

Cream of Broccoli Soup

This make-in-minutes soup is equally delicious made with fresh asparagus. May be served hot or cold.

1½	lb	broccoli, tough ends trimmed	700	g
1		stalk celery, thinly sliced	1	
1		small onion, chopped	1	
3	cups	chicken stock	750	mL
⅛	tsp	dry mustard	.5	mL
		salt and pepper to taste		
1	cup	light cream	250	mL
		thin slices of lemon		

Combine first 4 ingredients in saucepan, bring to boil and simmer 10 minutes or until broccoli is just tender. Pour into blender or food processor, add mustard and salt and blend until smooth. Return to saucepan. Add cream and heat. Serve with a thin slice of lemon in each cup or bowl.
Note: Process only small amounts in blender to avoid the possibility of scalding.
Serves 6.

Goulash Soup

Hearty enough for a main course with sourdough rye bread.

1	lb	round steak, braising tips or lean stewing beef in small cubes	500	g
		flour		
3	Tbsp	oil	45	mL
3		medium onions, chopped	3	
1	tsp	salt	5	mL
½	tsp	freshly ground pepper	2	mL
½	tsp	marjoram	2	mL
½	tsp	savory	2	mL
		cayenne, to taste		
2	tsp	paprika	10	mL
3	Tbsp	tomato paste	45	mL
1	cup	beef bouillon	250	mL
1	cup	water	250	mL
1		can (14oz/398mL) stewed tomatoes	1	
2 or 3		potatoes, cut in eights	2 or 3	
½	cup	green pepper, chopped	125	mL

Dredge meat in flour. Heat oil in large, heavy saucepan or dutch oven. Brown meat, add onions and saute until golden brown. Add next 10 ingredients. Cover and cook slowly 1½ hours, or until meat is nearly tender. Add potatoes and cook another ½ hour, adding green peppers for the last 5 minutes.
Serves 6.

Irv's Mother's Cabbage Soup

1		small cabbage, shredded	1
½		green pepper, diced	½
1		medium onion, chopped	1
1	tsp	salt	5 mL
1	tsp	pepper	5 mL
½	cup	ketchup	125 mL
2	cups	water	500 mL
1	lb	spareribs, in pieces	500 g
¼	cup	rice	50 mL
1	Tbsp	butter	15 mL
2	Tbsp	flour	30 mL

In large saucepan or dutch oven combine the first 8 ingredients. Bring to a boil and then simmer for ½ hour. Add rice and simmer for 15 minutes more. Make a roux by mixing butter and flour with cold water. Gently stir into soup. Bring back to boil for 1 minute.
Serves 4.

Carrot-Curry Soup

Don't leave out the chopped almonds - they add so much to the incredible flavour of this easy-to-make soup.

1		medium onion, chopped	1
2	Tbsp	butter	30 mL
4		carrots, peeled and thinly sliced	4
4	cups	chicken stock	1 L
1		strip lemon peel	1
2	tsp	sugar	10 mL
1	tsp	curry powder	5 mL
¼	tsp	salt	1 mL
		pepper to taste	
3	Tbsp	dry sherry	45 mL
		toasted chopped almonds	
		snipped chives	

In a medium saucepan, sauté onion in butter until limp. Add next 7 ingredients, cover and boil gently 15 minutes or until carrots are tender. Remove strip of peel and whirl soup in blender until smooth. Stir in sherry, correct the seasonings, and reheat. Garnish each bowl with a sprinkle of almonds and chives.
Note: Take caution with hot liquids in blender - whirl in several stages, holding lid down firmly.
Serves 4-6.

Hearty Hamburger Soup

A meal in a bowl to please the whole family.

3	Tbsp	butter	45 mL
1½	lbs	lean ground beef	750 g
1		can (28oz/796mL) tomatoes	1
2		cans (10oz/284mL) consommé	1
1		can (10oz/284mL) onion soup	1
4		medium carrots, thinly sliced	4
1	cup	celery	250 mL
½	cup	celery leaves, chopped	125 mL
¼	cup	parsley, chopped	50 mL
1		bay leaf	1
1	tsp	oregano	5 mL
2	cups	water	500 mL
		pepper to taste	
½	cup	elbow macaroni	125 mL

Sauté beef in butter until browned. Add remaining ingredients and simmer covered for 40 minutes, stirring occasionally. Add macaroni and simmer uncovered until cooked, 5 - 10 minutes. Any leftover vegetables may be added at this point.
Serves 6-8.

Ham and Cheese Soup

An excellent main dish soup.

¼	cup	butter or margarine	50 mL
1		medium onion, chopped	1
½	cup	chopped celery	125 mL
1		large carrot, grated	1
⅓	cup	flour	75 mL
2	tsp	dry mustard	10 mL
2		chicken bouillon cubes	2
1	cup	boiling water	250 mL
4	cups	milk, divided	1 L
2	cups	grated cheddar cheese	500 mL
2	cups	finely chopped broccoli	500 mL
1½	cups	diced cooked ham	375 mL
2	Tbsp	chopped parsley	30 mL

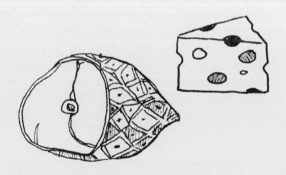

In a large heavy saucepan cook the first 4 ingredients until soft but not brown. Blend in the flour and mustard. Dissolve bouillon cubes in boiling water. Gradually add to cooked vegetables along with 1 cup of the milk. Cook, stirring until thickened. Add remaining milk and bring to a boil. Add remaining ingredients and heat through, being careful not to boil.
Serves 6-8.

Cheaty Soups

Leek and Stilton

1		pkg Knorr's Cream of Leek Soup	1
3	Tbsp	Stilton cheese, diced	45 mL

Make soup according to package directions. Just before serving add the cheese. Serve with additional Stilton cheese and pumpernickel bread. Serves 4.

Creamy Tomato

1		can (10oz/284mL) tomato soup	1
1		soup can milk	1
1		can (14oz/298 mL) tomatoes, broken up	1
		fresh or dried basil to taste	
2	Tbsp	butter	30 mL
		fresh parsley, chopped	
		croutons (optional)	

Combine all ingredients, except parsley and croutons, in a heavy saucepan. Cook and stir until hot. Ladle into soup bowls and sprinkle with parsley and croutons. Serves 4.

California Consommé

8	cups	chicken broth	2 L
2		avocados	2
2		lemons, thinly sliced	2
½	cup	sherry	125 mL
½	cup	chopped fresh parsley	125 mL

Heat broth to near boiling in saucepan. Place avocado slices (about ¼ avocado per person) and 2-3 lemon slices in bottom of each soup bowl. Ladle broth into bowls. Add 1 Tbsp (15mL) sherry to each serving. Sprinkle parsley on top.
Serves 6-8.

Crab Bisque

1	cup	crabmeat	250 mL
		sherry	
1		can (10oz/284mL) tomato soup	1
1		can (10oz/284mL) green pea soup	1
1		soup can cream or milk	1
		Worcestershire sauce to taste	

In the morning, put crabmeat in bowl and cover with sherry. Cover and refrigerate until ready to make soup. Combine last 4 ingredients in saucepan. Heat, add crabmeat and sherry.
Serves 4

A Fraudulent Frill

Turn a family favorite into company fare.

Thinly roll enough puff pastry to cover the top(s) of soup bowl(s). Bake at 425°F (220°C) for 12 to 15 minutes.

Spring Tonic

A refreshing soup - make well ahead, adding port and lemon juice before heating and serving.

2		cans (28oz/796mL) tomatoes	2	
2		stalks celery, with leaves	2	
2		carrots	2	
1		green pepper, seeded	1	
1		large onion	1	
3		peppercorns	3	
2		whole cloves	2	
1	tsp	salt	5	mL
½	tsp	basil	2	mL
½	tsp	sugar	2	mL
¼	cup	port	50	mL
1	Tbsp	fresh lemon juice	15	mL
		cheese croutons (optional)		

Pour tomatoes in a large saucepan, breaking up solid pieces. Cut vegetables into chunks and add to pot with spices and sugar. Cover, bring to a boil, then lower heat and simmer 1 hour, stirring once or twice. Cool. Strain the soup through a fine sieve and return bouillon to saucepan. Add port and lemon juice. Taste for seasoning. Bring to boil and serve, adding a few croutons to each bowl, if desired. Serves 6-8.

Salads

Nuts Over Crab

A delightfully different taste treat.

		butter lettuce		
¾	lb	crab	375	g
½	cup	pecans, broken, not chopped	125	mL

Dressing

½	cup	mayonnaise - not salad dressing	125	mL
3	Tbsp	fresh lime juice	45	mL
2	Tbsp	finely minced fresh dill	30	mL
		splash of white wine		

On 4 salad plates make a bed of butter lettuce leaves. Add more lettuce torn in bite size pieces. Arrange crab over the lettuce and top with broken pecans. Spoon dressing over. Enjoy!
Makes 4 luncheon size servings.

Mystery Salad

A refreshing luncheon salad.

1	cup	pineapple chunks	250	mL
2		green onions, finely chopped	2	
1	cup	cooked shrimp	250	mL
1	tsp	curry powder	5	mL
1	cup	diced celery	250	mL
1	cup	chopped lettuce	250	mL
1		large tomato, diced	1	
1	cup	mayonnaise	250	mL

To mayonnaise, add curry powder and let stand about an hour. Add remaining ingredients and chill. Serve on lettuce leaf and garnish with hard boiled egg slices.
Serves 4.

Two Rice Salad

A simple but very unusual salad.

⅔	cup	cooked wild rice	150 mL
1½	cups	cooked white rice	375 mL
¼	cup	pinenuts, lightly toasted	50 mL
¼	cup	dried apricots, coarsely chopped	50 mL
¼	cup	sesame oil dressing	50 mL
		pepper to taste	

Sesame Oil Dressing

½	cup	salad oil	125 mL
3	Tbsp	white wine vinegar	45 mL
1	Tbsp	minced parsley	15 mL
2	tsp	sesame seed oil	10 mL
¼	tsp	pepper	1 mL

Combine salad ingredients. Set aside. Mix together dressing ingredients and pour enough over salad so that it is well moistened. Cover and chill several hours. Salad will keep several days in the refrigerator.
Serves 8 as a side dish.

Beef and Horseradish Salad

For Sunday planned-overs!

        thin slices of rare roast beef or steak
        lettuce
        sliced tomatoes

Amounts will depend on appetites and whether it is served as a luncheon or dinner entrée.

Dressing

½	cup	plain yogurt	125 mL
2	Tbsp	mayonnaise	30 mL
1	Tbsp	chopped green onion	15 mL
1	Tbsp	horseradish	15 mL
1	Tbsp	chopped parsley	15 mL
1	tsp	lemon juice	5 mL
½	tsp	mustard	2 mL
½	tsp	Worcestershire sauce	2 mL
¼	tsp	Tabasco sauce	1 mL
		salt and pepper to taste	

Arrange lettuce, beef and tomato slices on each plate. Mix dressing ingredients in blender or food processor; pour over salad.
Dressing for 4 large servings.

Buffet Shrimp and Avocado

Many requests for this one!

1	lb	fresh shrimp	500	g
4		large stalks celery in ¼" dice	4	
1		large bunch green onions, chopped	1	
1	cup	alfalfa sprouts	250	mL
¾	cup	oil and vinegar dressing	175	mL
5-6		ripe avocados	5-6	

Combine first 5 ingredients. Cover and chill several hours. An hour before serving, peel and cut avocados into bite size pieces. Toss with first mixture. Add more dressing if there is not enough to thoroughly coat avocado.
Serves 12-14.

Emerald Salad

1		pkg lime gelatin	1	
¾	cup	hot water	175	mL
¾	cup	cold water	175	mL
¾	cup	grated unpeeled cucumber	175	mL
2	Tbsp	grated onion	30	mL
1	cup	cream style cottage cheese	250	mL
1	cup	mayonnaise	250	mL
⅓	cup	slivered almonds	75	mL

Dissolve gelatin in hot water; add cold water and refrigerate until slightly set. Drain cucumber and onion and add along with remaining ingredients to gelatin mixture. Pour into 4 cup (1L) mold and refrigerate until set.
Serves 6-8.

Jellied Shrimp Salad

Men like this, too!

1		envelope unflavored gelatin	1
¼	cup	water	50 mL
2	cups	shrimp	500 mL
1		can (19oz/540mL) tomatoes, broken up	1
1		onion, chopped	1
1	cup	mayonnaise	250 mL
2	Tbsp	hot dog relish	30 mL

Heat water and gelatin in saucepan; stir until gelatin is dissolved. Drain tomatoes and combine with all other ingredients. Stir in gelatin mixture. Pour into mold. A buffet salad that can also be sliced and served on a lettuce leaf as a starter.
Serves 6-8.

Mme Benoit's Potato Salad

4	cups	potatoes, sliced	1000 mL
2	Tbsp	hot consommé	30 mL
1½	tsp	salt	7 mL
¼	tsp	each, dry mustard and Dijon mustard	1 mL
2	Tbsp	green onions, chopped	30 mL
1	Tbsp	chopped parsley	15 mL
2	Tbsp	wine or cider vinegar	30 mL
5	Tbsp	olive or vegetable oil	75 mL

Cook potatoes; drain; put back in pan over high heat for a few minutes to dry water out. Pour consommé over potatoes and mix so that liquid is absorbed. Make a dressing, using last 7 ingredients. Add to potatoes. Will keep covered in refrigerator 3-4 days.
Serves 6.

Spinach Salad With A Difference

Fabulous!

1	lb	(about 2 bunches) fresh spinach, trimmed, washed and dried	500	g
6		large mushrooms, sliced	6	
1	cup	sliced water chestnuts	250	mL
8		slices bacon, cooked crisp, drained and crumbled	8	
¾	cup	fresh bean sprouts	175	mL
⅔	cups	shredded Gruyère or Emmenthal cheese	150	mL
⅓	cup	thinly sliced red onion	75	mL

Toss and serve with the following dressing which makes the difference.

Chutney Dressing

¼	cup	red wine vinegar	50	mL
2-3	Tbsp	Major Grey's chutney, diced	30-45	mL
1-2		garlic cloves, crushed	1-2	
2	Tbsp	coarsely ground French mustard	30	mL
2	tsp	sugar	10	mL
½-¾	cup	vegetable oil salt, freshly ground pepper	125-175	mL

Combine first 5 ingredients in blender or food processor and mix until smooth. With machine running, slowly pour in oil until thick and smooth. Taste and season, adjusting chutney and/or oil, if necessary. Refrigerate. Let stand at room tempature 30 minutes before adding to salad.
Serves 8-10.

Indonesian Salad

A colorful variety of steamed and raw vegetables with a tangy peanut sauce makes this dish a welcome change. It is a meal in itself.

1	lb	snow peas or fresh green beans	500	g
3		small carrots cut in julienne strips	3	
½		small cabbage, coarsely shredded	½	
1		small stalk broccoli, cut into florets	1	
1	cup	bean sprouts	250	mL
1		cucumber, sliced	1	
8	oz	tofu, diced in small cubes	250	g
2		green onions, chopped	2	
2		hard-cooked eggs, sliced	2	

Steam first 4 ingredients separately until crisp tender. Rinse and drain well. (May be prepared ahead of time.) Arrange vegetables along with next 3 ingredients on large serving platter. Garnish with green onions and eggs. Pour warm peanut sauce over top.

Peanut Sauce

1	cup	dry roasted peanuts	250	mL
1	Tbsp	oil	15	mL
1		medium onion, chopped	1	
3		garlic cloves, minced	3	
1	Tbsp	sambal oelek (hot pepper sauce) or 4 hot chile peppers, chopped	15	mL
1		bay leaf	1	
2	Tbsp	lime juice	30	mL
2	Tbsp	kecap manis (sweet soy sauce)	30	mL
½	tsp	grated fresh ginger root	2	mL
2	Tbsp	coconut cream	30	mL
2	cups	chicken stock or water (approx.)	500	mL

Grind peanuts in blender or food processor. Sauté onion, garlic and sambal until soft. Add peanuts, the remaining ingredients, and ½ of the chicken stock. Simmer until sauce thickens. Add additional stock so that sauce is of pouring consistency. Serve with sates or salads.
Note: Coconut cream may be purchased in cans. It can also be made by steeping unsweetened shredded coconut in hot milk, then straining through a sieve, pressing out all the liquid.
Makes about 2 cups dressing.

Salad à la Cité

Can be a meal in itself.

sliced raw carrots
sliced celery
romaine
watercress
spinach leaves
beet tops
hard boiled eggs
tomatoes
smoked salmon

Combine ingredients in bowl. Amounts will be determined by the number to be served (e.g. ¼carrot, 2 romaine leaves, ½egg, ½tomato, 1oz smoked salmon etc. per person) or by what you have on hand. Toss with dressing.

Dressing

⅔	cup	olive oil	150	mL
⅓	cup	tarragon vinegar	75	mL
1	tsp	Dijon mustard	5	mL
		salt and pepper to taste		
½	tsp	garlic powder	2	mL

Makes 1 cup (250mL) dressing.

Marinated Zucchini Salad

Busy tomorrow? Make it tonight.

3	cups	unpeeled zucchini in ½" (1cm) slices	750 mL
2		medium tomatoes, diced	2
1	cup	mushrooms, sliced	250 mL
2	Tbsp	green onions, chopped	30 mL
½	cup	white vinegar	125 mL
⅓	cup	olive or salad oil	75 mL
1	Tbsp	sugar	15 mL
		salt and pepper	
½	tsp	basil	2 mL
¼	tsp	garlic powder	1 mL
		shredded mozzarella cheese	

Combine first 4 ingredients and place in a shallow dish. Combine remaining ingredients in jar; shake well; pour over vegetables. Cover and refrigerate overnight. Before serving, drain vegetables and place them in a bowl lined with lettuce leaves. Top with shredded mozzarella cheese.
Serves 8.

Zucchini Tabbouleh

2	cups	bulgar wheat	500 mL
4	cups	boiling water	1000 mL
2	cups	minced parsley	500 mL
½	cup	minced fresh mint	125 mL
⅔	cup	finely chopped green onion	150 mL
2	cups	diced zucchini	500 mL
1		cucumber, peeled and diced	1
½	cup	olive oil	125 mL
⅓-½	cup	lemon juice	75-125 mL
½	tsp	allspice	2 mL
		salt and pepper	

Put bulgar in bowl and add boiling water. Let stand 1 hour, drain off excess liquid. Add rest of ingredients and chill well. Serve as is in Pita bread or as a salad on a lettuce leaf.
Note: Add sour cream to bind mixture when stuffing Pita bread.
Also: Delicious with chopped tomatoes, when in season, and sprouts. Serves 8.

Mary's French Dressing

½	cup	oil	125	mL
⅓	cup	sugar	75	mL
¼	cup	white vinegar	50	mL
¼	cup	ketchup	50	mL
½	tsp	dry mustard	2	mL
½	tsp	salt	2	mL
½	tsp	pepper	2	mL
		juice of ½ lemon		
½		medium onion, peeled	½	

Combine all ingredients in a screw top jar. Cover and shake well. Leave onion in the dressing for several hours then remove. Store in refrigerator. Makes about 1 ½ cups of dressing (375mL).

Soy Sauce Vinegrette

Lovely served on a spinach and bean sprout salad.

¼	cup	vegetable oil	50	mL
2	Tbsp	wine vinegar	30	mL
2	Tbsp	soy sauce	30	mL
¼	tsp	black pepper	1	mL
¼	tsp	ground ginger	1	mL
1		garlic clove, minced	1	

Mix all ingredients until well blended.
Makes about ½ cup (125mL) dressing

Blue Cheese Dressing

Nothing "Blue" about this zesty dressing.

1	cup	sour cream	250 mL
1	cup	mayonnaise	250 mL
½		pkg (1½oz/42g) onion soup mix	½
¼	cup	sweet pickle juice	50 mL
½-1	cup	grated cheddar cheese	125-250 mL
1	cup	chopped blue or Roquefort cheese	250 mL
		chopped chives	

Put ingredients into blender or food processor and blend until smooth. Thin with milk to use.
Makes about 4 cups (1L).

Cora's Caesar Dressing

2		garlic cloves, minced	2
1		egg	1
⅓	cup	olive or vegetable oil	75 mL
⅓	cup	grated parmesan cheese	75 mL
2	Tbsp	vinegar	30 mL
1	tsp	Worcestershire sauce	5 mL
½	tsp	Dijon mustard	2 mL

Whisk ingredients together and store covered in the refrigerator.
Makes about ¾ cup (175mL) dressing.

Yogurt Dressings For Fruit

Three distinctive ways to dress up fresh fruit.

Dressing #1

2		eggs, well beaten	2	
2	Tbsp	sugar	30	mL
½	cup	pineapple juice	125	mL
1	cup	plain yogurt	250	mL
		lemon juice to taste		

In a double boiler cook the first 3 ingredients, stirring until slightly thickened. Cool. Mix in next two ingredients. Chill.
Makes 3 cups.

Dressing #2

1		small carton plain yogurt	1	
1-2	tsp	frozen orange juice concentrate	5-10	mL
		dash of vanilla		

Blend ingredients and toss with fresh fruit.
Makes 1 cup.

Dressing #3

⅔	cup	toasted unsweetened coconut	150	mL
1	cup	yogurt	250	mL
¼	cup	maple syrup	75	mL

Combine ingredients and chill. Serve over fresh fruit salad.
Makes 2 cups.

Entrées   Luncheon - Dinner

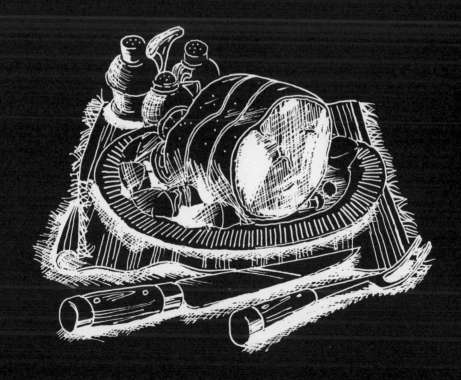

Quiche Me Quick

1		can (8oz/227mL) crushed pineapple	1
¾	cup	shredded Swiss cheese	175 mL
⅔	cup	milk	150 mL
2		eggs, beaten	2
2	Tbsp	chopped green onion	30 mL
1	Tbsp	Dijon mustard	15 mL
⅛	tsp	garlic salt	.5 mL
¼	cup	buttermilk baking mix	50 mL
2	Tbsp	grated parmesan cheese	30 mL

Preheat oven to 350°F (180°C). Drain pineapple. Combine all ingredients except parmesan cheese; pour into 2 buttered 1 cup baking dishes (I use onion soup bowls). Sprinkle 1 Tbsp (15mL) of parmesan cheese over each dish.
Bake 50-60 minutes; let stand 5 minutes before serving.
Serves 2.

Perennial Boar

1½	lb	pork tenderloin	750 g
2	Tbsp	butter	30 mL
1	cup	whipping cream	250 mL
¼	cup	dry white wine	50 mL
¼	cup	brandy	50 mL
3	Tbsp	Dijon mustard	45 mL
		dash ground pepper	

Cut meat into ½" (2cm) slices and pound to flatten. Sauté in butter until golden (about 6 minutes). Remove meat to platter. In same frypan add rest of ingredients and boil vigorously until sauce is thick enough to coat the back of a spoon (2-4 minutes). Return meat to pan and cover with sauce. Serves 4-6.

Taco Salad

1	lb	ground beef	500	g
1		can (14oz/398mL) red kidney beans	1	
1		head of lettuce	1	
1		medium onion, diced	1	
4		medium tomatoes, diced	4	
4	oz	grated cheese	125	g
½	cup	thousand island dressing	125	mL
1		medium size bag taco flavored chips or fritos	1	

Brown beef and drain off fat. Add beans and keep warm. Tear lettuce into bite size pieces. Add tomatoes, onions and cheese. Break chips into bite size pieces by flattening the bag with your hand. Add chips and dressing to lettuce. Toss. When ready to serve, add meat mixture and toss.
Serves 4 to 6.

Crab Crêpes Gratin

12		cooked crêpes, 6-7" in diameter	12

Filling

2	Tbsp	butter	30 mL
3	Tbsp	minced green onions	45 mL
2		medium tomatoes, finely chopped	2
1¾	cups	diced crabmeat or other cooked shellfish	425 mL
1	tsp	minced parsley	5 mL
¼	cup	dry white wine	50 mL
		salt and pepper to taste	
		juice of half a lemon	

Wine and Cheese Sauce

⅓	cup	dry white wine (or vermouth)	75 mL
2	Tbsp	cornstarch, blended in small bowl with 2 Tbsp (30mL) milk	30 mL
1½	cups	whipping cream	375 mL
¼	tsp	salt	1 mL
¼	tsp	white pepper	1 mL
½	cup	grated Swiss cheese	125 mL

Topping

¼	cup	grated Swiss cheese	50 mL
2	Tbsp	butter	30 mL

For filling heat butter in skillet and add the next 4 ingredients. Toss and stir over high heat for 1 minute. Add wine, salt and pepper and boil rapidly until liquid has almost entirely evaporated. Place in a bowl, stir in lemon juice and refrigerate until crêpes are ready to fill.

For sauce add wine to skillet and boil until reduced to 1 Tbsp. Remove from heat and stir in all ingredients but the cheese. Simmer for 2 minutes, stirring constantly. Stir in cheese and simmer until medium thick.

To assemble blend half the sauce into shellfish mixture, then place a big spoonful of the shellfish on lower third of each crêpe and roll. Arrange in buttered baking dish. Spoon over rest of sauce, sprinkle with the cheese and dab with bits of butter. Refrigerate until ready to bake.
Bake at 425°F (220°C) for 15 to 20 minutes in upper third of a preheated oven until hot and lightly browned.
Serves 4-6.

Quick Curried Seafood

Has the distinctive flavor of the east, but is light, and takes just minutes to make!

3	Tbsp	butter or margarine	45 mL
3	Tbsp	curry powder	45 mL
1		can (10oz/284mL) cream of mushroom soup	1
3	cups	sour cream	750 mL
¾	cup	chopped green onions	175 mL
1	lb	small scallops, shrimp or other cooked seafood	500 g

In top of double boiler melt butter; add curry and heat 5 minutes. Add remaining ingredients and cook until hot. Serve in patty shells or over cooked rice.
Serves 6-8.

South Seas Pork

3½	lb	cubed lean pork	1.5	kg
2		eggs, slightly beaten	2	
1½	cups	flour	325	mL
1	tsp	salt	5	mL
½	tsp	pepper	2	mL
2		cans (14oz/398mL) pineapple chunks	2	
2	cups	chicken bouillon	500	mL
¼	cup	soy sauce	50	mL
¼	cup	cornstarch	50	mL
2		green peppers, in chunks	2	

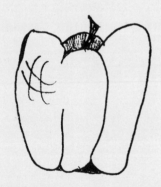

Preheat oven to 400°F (200°C). Combine flour, salt and pepper. Dip pork into egg and then into flour. Pour small amount of oil into large roasting pan. Add pork and stir to coat pieces with oil.
Bake until meat is browned, about 45 minutes.
Drain pineapple liquid into bowl, reserving chunks until later. Add next 3 ingredients to juice and mix well. Pour over meat and bake covered at 325°F (165°C) about 45 minutes. Add reserved pineapple and green pepper. Heat. Serve with oven baked rice.
Serves 8.

Sweet'n'Sour Shrimp

1	lb	large shrimp or prawns	500 g
		oil for deep frying	

Batter

1		egg	1
½	tsp	salt	2 mL
½	cup	sifted flour	125 mL
2	Tbsp	water	30 mL

Sauce

1	cup	vinegar	250 mL
1	cup	water	250 mL
½	tsp	salt	2 mL
1	cup	brown sugar	250 mL
3	Tbsp	ketchup	45 mL
¼	tsp	pepper	1 mL
2	cups	chopped pineapple	500 mL
2		large green peppers cut diagonally in 8 pieces	2
2		large tomatoes cut in 6 wedges	2
1	Tbsp	cornstarch	15 mL

Split shrimp along back but do not cut all the way through. Beat egg, add flour, salt and water and beat until smooth. Dip shrimp in the batter, fry in hot oil until golden brown. Combine remaining ingredients, except cornstarch, in a large saucepan and bring to a boil. Mix cornstarch with 2 Tbsp water. Stir carefully into sauce. Cook until thickened. Add shrimp. Bring to a boil and cook 1 minute. Serve immediately over rice with Chinese vegetables.

Shrimp Creole

½		green pepper, diced	½
1		slice (1"/2cm) onion, chopped	1
1		stalk celery, chopped	1
3	Tbsp	butter	45 mL
1	Tbsp	flour	15 mL
1		can (28oz/796mL) tomatoes	1
½	tsp	salt	2 mL
1	tsp	sugar	5 mL
½	tsp	curry powder	2 mL
1		sprig of parsley, chopped (or 1Tbsp/15mL dried flakes)	1
¾	lb	shrimp	375 g
		Worcestershire sauce	

Sauté first 3 ingredients in butter for 5 minutes. Add flour and blend. Add next 5 ingredients and simmer for 30 minutes. Stir in shrimp and Worcestershire sauce. Serve with hot rice.
Serves 6.

Shrimp or Chicken Casserole

12	oz	green spinach noodles, cooked al dente	375	mL
4		green onions, finely chopped	4	
2	lb	cooked shrimp or 4 cups cubed cooked chicken	1	kg
1½	cups	coarsely chopped mushrooms	375	mL
1	cup	sour cream	250	mL
1	cup	mayonnaise	250	mL
1	cup	whipping cream	250	mL
¼	cup	dry sherry	50	mL
1	tsp	Dijon mustard	5	mL
		salt, freshly ground pepper		
1	cup	grated sharp cheddar cheese (Ingersol recommended)	250	mL

Preheat oven to 350°F (180°C). Place noodles and green onions in 13x9" (34x22cm) casserole dish. Cover with shrimp or chicken and mushrooms. Combine next 6 ingredients and pour over chicken. Sprinkle with grated cheese.
Bake covered for 30 minutes or until bubbly. Uncover for last 10 minutes of cooking.
Serves 6-8.

Ham En Croute

Leftover ham has never been so glamorous!

1		pkg frozen puff pastry	1
Filling			
2	Tbsp	butter	30 mL
½	cup	chopped green onions	125 mL
½	lb	mushrooms, sliced	250 g
2	Tbsp	flour	30 mL
½	cup	heavy cream	125 mL
2	cups	diced cooked ham	500 mL
1	cup	diced Swiss cheese	250 mL

Remove puff pastry from freezer 1 hour prior to assembly.
Preheat oven to 375°F (190°C). To prepare filling, cook onion and mushrooms in butter until onions are soft. Sprinkle in flour, cook 1 minute. Gradually stir in cream. Cook and stir until thickened. Cool. Stir in ham and cheese.
Roll pastry to a 14" (36cm) square. Spread filling over dough to within 1" (2.5cm) of edges. Fold in edges of pastry. Roll up as for a jelly roll. Place seam side down on a lightly greased baking sheet. Brush with egg wash (egg yolk mixed with water).
Bake for 35 minutes.
Note: The puff pastry recipe with "Greek Meat Loaf" may be substituted in this recipe.
Serves 6.

Chicken Royale

This recipe provides a delicious sauce for rice.

4		chicken breasts, halved	4
⅓	cup	butter	75 mL
1	tsp	salt	5 mL
2	tsp	paprika	10 mL
½	tsp	pepper	2 mL
½	cup	finely chopped onion	125 mL
2	cups	sliced mushrooms	500 mL
¾	cup	dry white wine	175 mL
2		cans (10oz/284mL) cream of chicken soup	2
½	tsp	Tabasco	2 mL
½	cup	red currant jelly	125 mL

Preheat oven to 325°F (160°C). Brown chicken in skillet, sprinkle with seasonings. Add onions and mushrooms and when slightly browned add rest of ingredients mixing well. Place in casserole dish and cover for half baking time.
Bake for 1 to 1½ hours.
Serves 8.

Paella à la Valenciana

¼	cup	olive oil	50	mL
1		frying chicken, cut in serving pieces	1	
¼	lb	veal, cubes	125	g
¼	lb	lean pork, cubes	125	g
2		garlic cloves, minced	2	
1		onion, finely chopped	1	
2	tsp	salt	10	mL
¼	tsp	pepper	1	mL
3		large tomatoes, peeled and chopped	3	
2	cups	uncooked rice	500	mL
4	cups	water	1	L
1	cup	dry white wine	250	mL
1		sweet red pepper, chopped	1	
1		pkg (10oz/300g) frozen peas	1	
1		pkg (10oz/300g) frozen artichoke hearts	1	
1		garlic clove, minced	1	
4-5	cups	shellfish (lobster, crabmeat, shrimp, seafood delight) fresh, cooked or canned	1-1½	L

Garnish

8-10		cherrystone clams, cooked, in the shell	8-10	
8-10		mussels, cooked, in the shell	8-10	
12		asparagus tips, cooked, fresh or canned	12	
		pimento strips		

In heavy, deep skillet, brown the chicken, veal and pork in olive oil. Add the next 5 ingredients. Cover and cook for 10 minutes. Add next 7 ingredients. Cover and cook gently for 20 minutes. Add seafood. Stir mixture well and cook to combine, making sure rice is cooked, no more than 10 minutes.
To serve: arrange rice mixture in shallow paella or casserole dish. Place open mussels and clams in their shells on top of rice and garnish with asparagus and strips of pimento.
Note: If fresh mussels and clams are unavailable, use canned. If rice appears dry, add a little more wine
Serves 8-10.

Veal Chops à la Wendy

Absolutely delicious!

4		veal loin chops, at least 1" (2cm) thick. May use cheaper cut. salt and pepper	4	
2	Tbsp	butter	30	mL
¼	cup	onion, chopped	50	mL
2	cups	fresh, coarse, breadcrumbs	500	mL
¾-1	cup	grated parmesan cheese	175-250	mL
2	Tbsp	butter, melted	30	mL
¾-1	cup	white wine	175-250	mL

Preheat oven to 400°F (200°C). Choose a baking pan that the meat will fill when placed in a single layer. Melt butter in pan, sprinkle with onion. Place meat on top. Combine crumbs with cheese; cover meat so that it is "sealed." Sprinkle with melted butter; pour wine over all. Bake 1-1½ hours, until tender. Add extra wine if it becomes too dry.
Serves 4.

Peppered Roast Beef

Perfect for the buffet!

4-6	lb	top round beef roast	2-3	kg
3		garlic cloves, peeled and cut into slivers	3	
		cracked or coarsely ground pepper		

Preheat oven to 500°F (260°C). Make 1" (2cm) deep incisions all over roast and insert slivers of garlic. Sprinkle meat generously with pepper; place in roasting pan fat side up.
Roast, allowing 7 minutes per pound for medium rare. Turn off heat and leave roast in oven for 2 hours longer **without opening oven door.** Serve warm or chill for several hours. Bring to room temperature before slicing.
Serves 8-10.

Veal Scallops in Creamy Sauce

12		thin slices of veal	12	
2	Tbsp	butter	30	mL
		flour		

Sauce

¼	cup	chopped mushrooms	50	mL
½	cup	bouillon	125	mL
½	cup	whipping cream	125	mL
3	Tbsp	white wine	45	mL

Dredge veal in flour and sear in butter in hot frying pan. Add sauce ingredients to pan. Reduce until thick; add chopped parsely; pour over veal.
Serves 3-4.

Vitello Tonnato

Don't hesitate! This unusual combination is tasty and elegant.

3	lb	boneless veal roast, rolled and tied	1.5	kg
2		garlic cloves, slivered	2	
4	cups	chicken stock	1	L
2	cups	dry white wine	500	mL
1		onion, chopped	1	
2		carrots, chopped	2	
2		celery stalks, chopped	2	
1		bay leaf	1	
		peel of a lemon		
10		whole peppercorns	10	

Tuna Sauce

1		can (6.5oz/184g) tuna, drained	1	
1		can (2oz/50g) anchovy fillets, drained and rinsed	1	
2	Tbsp	lemon juice	30	mL
2	cups	mayonnaise	500	mL

Garnish

1		small jar of capers	1	
1		lemon, seeded and thinly sliced	1	
2	Tbsp	parsley, chopped	30	mL
12		black olives	12	

Make deep incisions in veal; insert garlic slivers. Place roast in heavy saucepan; add next 8 ingredients. Bring to a boil; reduce heat; simmer partially covered for 1½ - 2 hours or until meat is tender. Remove from heat; allow veal to cool in liquid in pan. Remove veal; strain liquid; reduce on high heat to ½ cup (125mL).

Sauce
Mash tuna, anchovies, and lemon juice in a small bowl. Slowly blend in mayonnaise. Add the reduced veal stock and blend.

Carve veal into thin slices; nap with sauce; cover with plastic wrap; refrigerate for at least 3 hours or overnight. Serve at room temperature, garnished with last 4 ingredients.
Serves 6-8.

Brochette of Pork

| 2½ | lb | boneless loin of pork, trimmed and cut into ½" (1.5cm) cubes | 1.2 k |

Marinade

¼	cup	soy sauce	50 mL
½	cup	water	125 mL
¼	cup	honey	50 mL
2	Tbsp	red wine vinegar	30 mL
1	Tbsp	finely chopped garlic	15 mL
1	Tbsp	freshly grated ginger	15 mL
		salt to taste	
1	tsp	paprika	5 mL
1	Tbsp	lemon juice	15 mL
¼	cup	butter	50 mL
1	Tbsp	coriander (optional)	15 mL

Combine first 8 ingredients of marinade. Marinate pork for 4 hours or more (best overnight). Thread pork onto skewers for barbeque. To the marinade add lemon juice, butter and coriander and heat on stove until thickened. This sauce is excellent as a dip for meat.
Serves 6-8.

Marinated Pork Roast

4-5	lb	pork loin roast, boned and tied	2	kg

Marinade

½	cup	soy sauce	125	mL
½	cup	sherry	125	mL
3		garlic cloves, minced	3	
2	tsp	dry mustard	10	mL
1	tsp	thyme	5	mL
¾	tsp	ground ginger	3	mL

Sherry Sauce

1¼	cup	currant jelly	300	mL
2	Tbsp	sherry	30	mL
1	Tbsp	soy sauce	15	mL

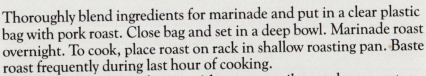

Thoroughly blend ingredients for marinade and put in a clear plastic bag with pork roast. Close bag and set in a deep bowl. Marinade roast overnight. To cook, place roast on rack in shallow roasting pan. Baste roast frequently during last hour of cooking.
Bake at 325°F (160°C) for 2½ - 3 hours or until meat thermometer registers 170°F (85°C).
Serve with sherry sauce: in saucepan, heat jelly until melted. Stir in sherry and soy sauce and simmer for a few minutes.
Serves 10-12.

Greek Meatloaf

Puff Pastry

¾	cup	flour	175	mL
½	cup	unsalted butter	125	mL
¼	cup	sour cream	50	mL

Filling

3	Tbsp	oil	45	mL
1		medium onion, finely chopped	1	
1		garlic clove, minced	1	
2		peppers (1 green and 1 red if available) finely chopped	2	
1	lb	lean ground beef	500	g
½	cup	soft breadcrumbs	125	mL
1		egg	1	
2	Tbsp	tomato ketchup	30	mL
1	tsp	salt	5	mL
½	tsp	pepper	2	mL
1½	tsp	oregano	7	mL
1	tsp	thyme	5	mL
4	oz	feta cheese (or mozzarella)	115	g
1		egg yolk	1	
1	Tbsp	water	15	mL

For pastry cut butter into flour until mixture resembles coarse meal. Blend in sour cream. Roll out into a large rectangle.

For filling cook first 4 ingredients in a skillet until soft. Cool. Combine with next 8 ingredients. Spread meat mixture over dough to within 1 inch of edge. Sprinkle with feta cheese and roll up like a jelly roll. Make sure sides are well closed. Brush with egg wash (egg yolk mixed with water). At this stage, roll can be refrigerated or frozen for later use. Chill at least 20 minutes before cooking.

Bake at 425°F (220°C) for 10 minutes. Reduce temperature to 375°F (190°C) and bake for 25 minutes or until golden. Remove from oven and let cool for about 5 minutes. Cut into slices and serve with a salad.

Note: The pastry may have to be covered with tin foil to prevent roll getting too brown during baking.

Serves 6.

Henri's Leg of Lamb

Our New Year's Eve treat!

1		leg of lamb, boned	1	
⅔	cup	olive oil	150	mL
3	Tbsp	lemon juice	45	mL
1	tsp	oregano	5	mL
1	cup	onions, thinly sliced	250	mL
3		garlic cloves, sliced	3	
2	Tbsp	parsley, chopped	30	mL
1	tsp	salt	5	mL
½	tsp	pepper	2	mL
3		bay leaves, crumbled	3	

Cut away any fat or fell left on leg of lamb. Combine all other ingredients; marinate lamb for 12-24 hours at room temperature or up to 3 days in refrigerator. Let come to room temperature. Preheat broiler. Lay lamb on rack fat side down, sprinkle with salt.
Broil 15 minutes; turn and broil for another 15 minutes or less.
Serves 4-6.

Honey-Lemon Chicken

2		chicken breasts, skinned and halved (thighs may also be used) flour, dash ginger, black pepper	2
2	Tbsp	butter	30 mL
2	Tbsp	soy sauce	30 mL
¼	cup	lemon juice	50 mL
¼	cup	honey	50 mL

Preheat oven to 350°F (180°C). Shake chicken in flour mixture until well coated. Place in baking dish in single layer. Bake for 30 minutes.
Prepare sauce by mixing the next 4 ingredients in saucepan and heating until combined. Pour over chicken and bake for additional 30 minutes, basting several times.
Serves 4.

Orange Chicken

A fresh fruity taste!

3		chicken breasts, skinned, boned and halved flour, salt, pepper	3
¼	cup	butter	50 mL
½	cup	chopped onion	125 mL
½	cup	orange juice concentrate	125 mL
½	cup	vermouth orange slices, parsley and slivered almonds for garnish	125 mL

Dust chicken with flour, salt, and pepper. Brown lightly in butter. Add remaining ingredients. Cover tightly and simmer 20 minutes. Remove to serving platter. Spoon sauce over chicken. Garnish with orange slices, parsley, and almonds. Sauce may be doubled for serving with rice.
Serves 4-6.

Chicken with Herbed Carrot Sauce

Different! Chicken melts in your mouth.

1		large chicken breast boned and halved	1
		flour	
3	Tbsp	butter or margarine	45 mL
1	cup	grated carrot	250 mL
¼	cup	minced onion	50 mL
1	tsp	chives and/or parsley	5 mL
¼	tsp	basil	1 mL
2	Tbsp	cognac or brandy	30 mL
1	Tbsp	unsalted butter	15 mL
1	Tbsp	flour	15 mL
1	cup	chicken stock	250 mL
¼	tsp	cayenne pepper	1 mL
1	Tbsp	white wine vinegar	15 mL
½	cup	heavy cream	125 mL

Preheat oven to 300°F (150°C). Dredge chicken in flour and salt and pepper to taste. Brown in butter in skillet; transfer to a casserole. Cook and stir next 4 ingredients in skillet; add to casserole. Sprinkle with cognac. Whisk butter and flour in skillet making a roux; cook for 2 minutes. Add next 3 ingredients and whisk until well mixed. Pour into casserole.
Bake, covered, for 40 minutes. Transfer chicken to platter; keep warm. Add cream to casserole; stir over heat until slightly thickened. Nap chicken with sauce and serve.
Serves 2.

Chicken Parmigiana

6		large chicken breasts, skinned, boned and halved	6
1½	tsp	salt, divided	7 mL
¼	tsp	pepper	1 mL
		flour	
2		eggs, beaten	2
2¼	cups	bread or cracker crumbs	550 mL
		shortening or oil	
3		medium onions, chopped	3
3		garlic cloves, minced	3
2		cans (19oz/540mL) whole tomatoes	2
⅓	cup	dry red wine	75 mL
1		bay leaf, crushed	1
1	tsp	oregano	5 mL
½	tsp	thyme	2 mL
1	lb	mozzarella cheese cut into 12 slices	500 g
½	cup	grated parmesan cheese	125 mL

Preheat oven to 400°F (200°C). Flatten chicken breasts slightly and sprinkle with ¾tsp salt and pepper. Dip in flour, then eggs, and then crumbs. Brown slowly until golden and done. Remove from pan. In shortening, sauté onions and garlic. Stir in next 5 ingredients and remaining ¾tsp salt. Simmer 15 minutes, stirring occasionally. Spoon half the sauce into a 13x9″ (34x22cm) baking dish. Cover with breasts. Place cheese slices between chicken pieces. Spoon on remaining sauce. Sprinkle with parmesan cheese. (At this point, dish may be wrapped and frozen. Thaw completely before baking. Bake about 15 minutes longer to heat through).
Bake for 15 minutes or until heated through.
Serves 12.

Chicken Dijon

4-6		chicken breasts, boned and skinned	4-6
⅓	cup	flour	75 mL
¼	tsp	salt	1 mL
¼	tsp	pepper	1 mL
¼	cup	butter or margarine	50 mL
2	Tbsp	brandy	30 mL
1		onion, finely chopped	1
⅓	cup	chopped fresh parsley	75 mL
½	cup	sliced mushrooms	125 mL
2	Tbsp	Dijon mustard	30 mL
2	Tbsp	lemon juice	30 mL
2	cups	half and half cream	500 mL
3		egg yolks, lightly beaten	3

Preheat oven to 375°F (190°C). Coat chicken in flour, salt and pepper. Brown in butter. Pour warmed brandy over and flame, shaking pan until flame dies. Remove chicken to a 2 qt (2L) casserole. Simmer next 3 ingredients in pan for about 4 minutes. In a saucepan combine mustard, lemon and cream and bring to a boil. Stir in onion, mushroom mixture and spoon over chicken. Cover casserole.
Bake for 45 minutes. Drain off sauce - stir into egg yolks. Simmer, stirring constantly, until thickened. Pour a little over the chicken. Pass the remainder in a gravy boat.
Serves 4-6.

Trout Meunière

For a dinner with good friends - best served from skillet to table.

4		rainbow trout	4
		milk	
		flour	
3	Tbsp	butter	45 mL
3	Tbsp	vegetable oil	45 mL
1		bunch green onions, chopped	1
½	cup	butter	125 mL
1	Tbsp	lemon juice	15 mL
¼	cup	white wine (optional)	50 mL
		salt and pepper	
		lemon wedges	

Dip fish in milk and then in flour. Fry in melted butter and oil 5-6 minutes each side or until delicately browned. Place on platter and keep warm. Sauté onions in butter for 5 minutes and stir in next 3 ingredients. Pour sauce over fish. Serve with lemon wedges. Serves 4.

Teriyaki Salmon

6		boneless salmon fillets	6
⅔	cup	teriyaki sauce	150 mL
2	Tbsp	lemon juice	30 mL
1	Tbsp	grated onion	15 mL
1	Tbsp	brown sugar	15 mL

Place salmon in a single layer in glass dish. Combine next 3 ingredients and pour over salmon. Marinate 1 hour at room temperature. Drain. Broil or barbeque salmon until nearly cooked; sprinkle brown sugar over top and cook until salmon just flakes. Serves 4-6.

Red Snapper and Crab in Wine

Delicious! And I don't like red snapper!

2		fillets (6oz/180g) of red snapper salt and pepper to taste flour	2
2	Tbsp	butter	30 mL
¼	cup	dry red wine	50 mL
¼	cup	fish stock or chicken bouillon	50 mL
2	Tbsp	butter splash lemon juice salt and pepper	30 mL
¼	cup	crabmeat	50 mL
		fresh basil (optional)	

Preheat oven to 350°F (180°C). Season fillets with salt and pepper. Dredge in flour and sauté in butter in hot skillet 2 minutes per side. Place fish in buttered baking dish. Deglaze skillet with wine, stirring vigorously with wooden spoon. Add stock, stir and simmer one minute. Pour sauce over fish and bake 10 minutes. Remove from oven; cover to keep warm. Turn oven to broil. In skillet heat and stir butter, lemon juice and seasonings until blended. Place crab on top of fish. Pour the lemon sauce over all. Broil momentarily to ensure crabmeat is hot. Garnish with basil.
Note: May substitute any large flaked fish with distinctive flavour e.g. sturgeon, cod, ling cod or bass.
Serves 2.

Sole Florentine

Sole with a zesty Mediterranean flavor.

1½	lb	spinach, cooked, drained, and chopped	750 g
¼	tsp	salt	1 mL
¼	tsp	pepper	1 mL
½	cup	light cream	125 mL
¼	cup	butter	50 mL
2	Tbsp	flour	30 mL
½	tsp	salt	2 mL
⅛	tsp	pepper	.5 mL
⅛	tsp	paprika	.5 mL
4		large sole fillets	4
2	Tbsp	cooking oil	30 mL
2	Tbsp	butter	30 mL
1	cup	grated cheddar cheese	250 mL
1		can(7½oz/213mL) tomato sauce	1

Preheat oven to 375°F (190°C). Mix together the first 5 ingredients and place in a greased 7x11″ (2L) baking dish. Combine flour, salt, pepper and paprika and dredge sole fillets to coat. Heat butter and oil in a heavy skillet and quickly sauté sole until golden on each side. Lay fish on spinach mixture; sprinkle with half of cheese. Pour tomato sauce over and sprinkle with remaining cheese.
Bake for 20 minutes or until hot and bubbly.
Serves 4.

Scallops in Crème Fraîche Sauce

1	cup	fish stock	250 mL
1	cup	white wine	250 mL
1		leek (white part only) cut in 1½" (4cm) julienne strips	1
1		carrot cut in 1½" (4cm) julienne strips	1
3-4		fresh mushrooms, thinly sliced	3-4
3	Tbsp	butter	45 mL
2	cups	pea pods cut in strips	500 mL
1	qt	scallops at room temperature, cut in quarters if using sea scallops	1 L
2	cups	crème fraîche juice of ½ lemon	500 mL

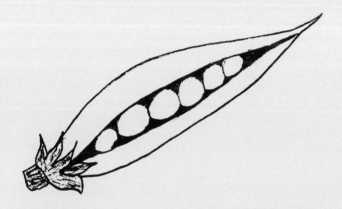

Combine stock and wine in small saucepan; bring to a boil and let simmer to reduce volume. Pour into casserole. Sauté the next 3 ingredients in butter 7 minutes. Add peapods, simmer for 3 minutes. Stir in crème fraîche and lemon juice. Add to casserole. Just before serving, heat sauce to **almost** boiling, stir in scallops and let sit for about 3 minutes. Serve.
If commercial crème fraîche is unavailable see index for recipe.
Serves 6-8.

Sole Fourées

This is very easy to prepare, especially the second time you make it! Filling can be made in the microwave to save time.

6		small fillets of sole	6	
¼	cup	butter, melted	50	mL
½	cup	fresh white breadcrumbs	125	mL

Filling

3	Tbsp	butter, divided	45	mL
2	Tbsp	flour	30	mL
¾	cup	hot milk	175	mL
¼-½	tsp	salt	1-2	mL
		white pepper to taste		
4	oz	cooked prawns	125	g
4	oz	mushrooms, quartered	125	g

Preheat oven to 350°F (180°C). Melt 1 Tbsp (15mL) of the butter for filling, and toss mushrooms in it for a minute or two. Remove mushrooms and reserve. Add remaining 2 Tbsp (30mL) butter, melt, add flour and cook roux a few minutes. Add hot milk all at once and whisk until smooth. Cook over medium-low heat, stirring until slightly thickened, about 8-10 minutes. Season to taste with salt and white pepper; add prawns and mushrooms. Put good spoonful of filling on each sole fillet and roll up. Place seam side down, in shallow, buttered, ovenproof dish. Pour any extra sauce around fish. Brush melted butter over fillets, sprinkle crumbs on top and drizzle with remainder of butter. Bake for 20 minutes. Garnish with watercress bouquets or parsley sprigs. Serves 3 as main course, 6 as an appetizer.

Vegetables

Broccoli Casserole

Make early in the day and bake before serving.

1½	lbs	fresh broccoli, cut up	750 g
1		can (10oz/284mL) cream of mushroom soup	1
½	cup	grated sharp cheddar cheese	125 mL
¼	cup	mayonnaise	50 mL
1	Tbsp	chopped pimento	15 mL
1½	tsp	lemon juice	7 mL
⅓	cup	cheese cracker crumbs	75 mL

Preheat oven to 350°F (180°C). Cook broccoli in boiling water until crisp tender, about 5 minutes. Drain. Turn into 1½ qt (1.5L) casserole. Combine remaining ingredients, except crumbs and pour over broccoli. Top with crumbs.
Bake for 35 minutes.
Serves 6-8.

Green Bean Casserole

2		pkgs (12oz/350g) frozen French style green beans	2
1		can (10oz/284mL) cream of mushroom soup	1
1		can (8oz/227mL) water chestnuts, sliced	1
1	cup	sliced mushrooms	250 mL
1		can (3oz/85g) french fried onions	1

Preheat oven to 350°F (180°C). Combine all ingredients, except onions. Place in casserole and bake 30 minutes or until beans are tender. Sprinkle onions on top; bake about 10 minutes more or until onions are piping hot.
Serves 6-8.

Green Beans, Viennese Style

3	lbs	green beans, sliced and cooked	1.5	kg
3	Tbsp	butter	45	mL
3	Tbsp	flour	45	mL
1		medium onion, chopped	1	
1	Tbsp	chopped dill	15	mL
½	tsp	chopped parsley	2	mL
½	cup	chicken broth or bouillon	125	mL
1	Tbsp	vinegar	15	mL
		dash salt and pepper		
1	cup	sour cream	250	mL

Melt butter. Blend in flour and onion and brown. Add dill, parsley and chicken broth. Bring to a boil. Add beans, vinegar, salt and pepper, and sour cream. Heat and serve.
Serves 10.

Delicious Squash Casserole

2	lbs	yellow squash	1	kg
½		large onion, cut in chunks	½	
1		can (10oz/284mL) cream of chicken soup	1	
1	cup	sour cream	250	mL
1	cup	grated carrots	250	mL
1		pkg (8oz/227g) herb seasoned stuffing mix	1	
½	cup	butter or margarine, melted	125	mL

Preheat oven to 350°F (180°C). Steam squash and onion until squash is crisp tender. Peel and cut squash in slices or chunks. Combine soup, sour cream and carrots. Fold in squash and onion. Combine stuffing mix with butter and spread half into casserole. Spoon vegetable mixture on top. Sprinkle with remaining stuffing.
Bake 25-30 minutes or until squash is fork tender.
Serves 6.

Zucchini Casserole

4		medium zucchini in ½" (1cm) diagonal slices	4	
2	Tbsp	butter, divided	30	mL
1		large onion, sliced	1	
2		large tomatoes in ½" (1cm) slices	2	
1	tsp	dried oregano	5	mL
1½	cups	grated sharp cheddar cheese	375	mL

Quickly sauté zucchini slices in half the butter, about 2 minutes. Place in a 1½ qt (1.5L) casserole. Sauté onion in remaining butter until cooked. Layer over zucchini. Top with tomato slices. Sprinkle with oregano and then with grated cheese. Refrigerate if made ahead. Bake 325°F (160°C) 30 minutes.
Serves 4-6.

Zucchini Italiana

Veggies for the barbeque.

2	zucchini, sliced	2
1	onion, sliced	1
4	mushrooms, sliced	4
½	green pepper, chopped	½
1	tomato, chopped	1
2	garlic cloves, minced	2
	butter	
	salt and pepper	

Combine ingredients except butter and seasonings, and divide onto 2 sheets of heavy foil. Dot with butter and season with salt and pepper. Seal foil tightly around vegetables and grill approximately 15 minutes on barbeque.
Serves 4.

Brussel Sprouts, Bon Vivant

A different vegetable dish, particularly nice with turkey or chicken.

1½	lbs	brussel sprouts, cooked in salted water with 2 tsp (10mL) grated onion	750 g
1	cup	boiled chestnuts (15 minutes), peeled and sliced (canned may be used)	250 mL
½	cup	prepared poultry dressing butter	125 mL
2	Tbsp	butter	30 mL
2	Tbsp	flour	30 mL
2	cups	milk	500 mL
⅓	cup	grated Swiss cheese nutmeg	75 mL

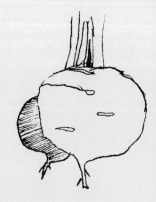

Preheat oven to 400°F (200°C). Prepare white sauce: melt butter in medium saucepan. Add flour and stir. Add milk gradually, continuing to stir. Cook until medium thick. Add Swiss cheese and nutmeg. Set aside. Sauté the poultry dressing and chestnuts in plenty of butter to coat well. In a buttered 9x13" (22x34cm) baking dish, layer half of the sprouts, poultry dressing and white sauce. Repeat layers. Grate additional cheese over the top.
Bake until cheese has melted and brussel sprouts are bubbly hot. Serves 6.

Big Potato Casserole

Wonderful for large gatherings!

1		pkg (2.2lb/1kg) frozen hash brown potatoes	1	
2	cups	sour cream	500	mL
1		medium onion, chopped	1	
2		cans (10oz/284mL) cream of mushroom soup	2	
1	cup	grated sharp cheddar cheese	250	mL
2	Tbsp	melted butter or margarine	30	mL
2	cups	crushed cornflakes	500	mL
½	cup	melted butter or margarine	125	mL

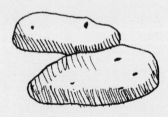

Preheat oven to 350°F (180°C). Combine potatoes and the next 5 ingredients in a large casserole dish or a 9x13" (34x22cm) pyrex dish. Top with cornflakes and butter.
Bake for 45-60 minutes.
Serves 10-12.

Oriental Peas

2	Tbsp	butter	30 mL
½	lb	mushrooms, sliced	250 g
4	cups	frozen peas	1 L
1		can (10oz/284mL) cream of mushroom soup	1
½	lb	bean sprouts	250 g
1		can (4oz/114mL) water chestnuts, sliced	1
⅓	cup	toasted slivered almonds	75 mL

Preheat oven to 350°F (180°C). Sauté mushrooms in butter. Combine with remaining ingredients and place in a 2 qt (1.5L) casserole. Bake for 20-25 minutes.
Serves 8-10.

Scalloped Cabbage

½		cabbage, shredded and cooked	½
1		can (10oz/284mL) cream of celery soup	1
20		soda crackers, crushed	20
¼	cup	butter	50 mL
¼	cup	grated parmesan cheese (optional)	50 mL

Preheat oven to 350°F (180°C). Combine cabbage and soup and place in a greased shallow 1 qt (1L) casserole. Sprinkle crumbs on top. Dot with butter. Sprinkle with cheese, if desired.
Bake 20 minutes or until top is golden.
Serves 4.

40 Carat Carrots

2	lbs	carrots, diagonally sliced	1	kg
1		large onion, sliced	1	
1		green pepper, sliced	1	
1		can (10oz/284mL) tomato soup	1	
2	Tbsp	ketchup	30	mL
½	cup	sugar	125	mL
½	cup	vinegar	125	mL
½	cup	vegetable oil	125	mL
1	tsp	salt	5	mL
⅛	tsp	pepper	.5	mL

Cook carrots in water until crisp tender. Drain. Separate onion into rings. Add to carrots with green pepper. Combine remaining 7 ingredients. Add to carrots and stir well to coat vegetables. Cover and refrigerate several hours or overnight. Serve chilled. Keeps in the refrigerator for several weeks.
Serves 8.

Onion Shortcake

1		medium onion, chopped	1
¼	cup	butter	50 mL
1¼	cups	corn muffin mix	300 mL
1		egg, beaten	1
⅓	cup	milk	75 mL
1	cup	cream style corn	250 mL
2		drops Tabasco Sauce	2
1	cup	sour cream	250 mL
¼	tsp	dill	1 mL
1	cup	grated sharp cheddar cheese	250 mL

Preheat oven to 425°F (220°C). Sauté onion in butter and set aside. Mix together the next 5 ingredients and spoon into an 8″ (20cm) square pan. Combine the sour cream, dill, half the cheese and the sautéed onion. Spread over batter. Sprinkle with remaining cheese.
Bake covered for the first 20 minutes; uncovered for 5-10 minutes more. Serves 8.

Tomatoes with Pine Nuts

Flavors of Italy - a wonderful side dish with pasta!

6		tomatoes	6	
		salt and pepper		
1	tsp	dried basil	5	mL
		or		
1	Tbsp	fresh basil	15	mL
2		garlic cloves, minced	2	
6	Tbsp	olive oil	90	mL
3	Tbsp	chopped parsley	45	mL
6	Tbsp	pine nuts	90	mL
3	Tbsp	melted butter	45	mL

Preheat oven to 350°F (180°C). Slice stem end off each tomato and remove the core, making a space at least half the depth of the tomato. Place in shallow baking dish. Sprinkle each tomato with salt, pepper, basil, garlic, and 1 Tbsp (15mL) of the oil.
Bake for 15 minutes.
Sprinkle tomatoes with parsley, nuts, and butter and bake for another 10 minutes. Serve hot or at room temperature.
Serves 6.

Carrot and Broccoli Timbale

2	cups	milk	500 mL
½	cup	butter	125 mL
1	cup	finely chopped onion	250 mL
2	Tbsp	butter	30 mL

Broccoli Layer

½	cup	grated Swiss cheese	125 mL
⅔	cup	breadcrumbs	150 mL
4		eggs	4
3	cups	puréed cooked broccoli	750 mL
½	tsp	basil	2 mL
¼	tsp	pepper	1 mL

Carrot Layer

½	cup	grated Swiss cheese	125 mL
⅔	cup	breadcrumbs	150 mL
6		eggs	6
3	cups	puréed cooked carrots	750 mL
½	tsp	nutmeg	2 mL
¼	tsp	pepper	1 mL

Bring milk and butter to a boil. Set aside. Sauté onions in butter until soft. Set aside. Prepare 2 pyrex loaf pans by buttering inside and lining with well buttered waxed paper.

Broccoli Layer
Mix broccoli layer ingredients. Add half of onion and half of milk. Mix again. Pour into prepared loaf pan and smooth top.

Carrot Layer
Mix carrot layer ingredients. Add remaining half of milk and onions. Mix again. Pour over broccoli layer. Place loaf pan in an oven dish. Pour hot water into dish so it reaches half way up sides of loaf pan.
Bake 325°F (160°C) for 40-45 minutes or until a knife inserted in centre comes out clean. Remove from oven. Let rest 10 minutes. Unmold and slice into serving pieces. Timbale may be made a day or two ahead, refrigerated and then reheated before serving.
Slices into 12 - ½" (1cm) thick servings.

Paw Paw Au Gratin

An excellent side dish with entrées that use other fruit, e.g., orange chicken.

2		papayas, peeled and seeds removed	2	
Cheese Sauce				
2	Tbsp	butter, melted	30	mL
2	Tbsp	flour	30	mL
2	tsp	dry mustard	10	mL
1	cup	milk	250	mL
½	cup	cheddar cheese, grated	125	mL
½	tsp	salt	2	mL
⅛	tsp	white pepper	.5	mL

Cut papaya into bite size pieces and set aside. In a saucepan stir flour and mustard into melted butter. Add milk slowly while stirring and cook until thickened. Add remaining ingredients and cook until cheese melts. Add papaya just before serving.
Serves 6-8.

Baked Corn Custard

3	Tbsp	butter	45	mL
1	tsp	minced onion	5	mL
2		leeks, finely chopped	2	
3	Tbsp	flour	45	mL
2	cups	milk	500	mL
1	cup	grated rattrap cheese	250	mL
1	tsp	sugar	5	mL
½	tsp	marjoram	2	mL
		salt and pepper to taste		
¼	cup	diced pimento	50	mL
2		eggs, beaten	2	
2		cans (14oz/398mL) niblet corn	2	
		breadcrumbs		
		butter		

Preheat oven to 350°F (180°C). Sauté leeks and onion in butter. Blend in flour. Add milk and cheese slowly. Add seasonings, pimento and sugar. Stir in corn and eggs. Put in buttered casserole (9x13"/22x34cm). Sprinkle top with breadcrumbs and dot with butter.
Bake for 35 minutes.
Serves 6.

Potato Tomato Bake

2	Tbsp	oil	30	mL
1	cup	chopped onions	250	mL
¼	cup	chopped green pepper	50	mL
¼	cup	chopped celery	50	mL
2	Tbsp	parsley	30	mL
1		clove garlic, minced	1	
½	tsp	basil	2	mL
1		bay leaf, crumbled	1	
1	tsp	salt	5	mL
1		can (14oz/500g) tomatoes	1	
4		large baking potatoes, unpared, sliced ¼" thick	4	
¼	cup	parmesan cheese	50	mL

Preheat oven to 400°F (200°C). Heat oil. Add onion, green pepper, celery, parsley, garlic, basil and bay leaf. Cook until onion is tender. Add salt and tomatoes. Layer ½ of potatoes in buttered dish. Then add ½ the sauce. Repeat layers. Sprinkle with parmesan. Cover with foil. Bake for 1¼ hours. Uncover and bake 15 minutes longer. Serves 6.

Frosted Cauliflower

Spectacular when served surrounded with steamed broccoli and cherry tomatoes.

1		medium head of cauliflower trimmed and left whole salt to taste	1
½	cup	mayonnaise	125 mL
2	tsp	Dijon mustard	10 mL
¾	cup	shredded sharp cheese	175 mL

Cook cauliflower in boiling water until crisp tender, 10 to 15 minutes. Drain and place in a shallow baking pan, sprinkle with salt. Combine mayonnaise and mustard and spread over cauliflower. Sprinkle with cheese.
Bake at 375°F (190°C) for 10 minutes or until cheese is melted.
Serves 6-8.

Vegetable Sauce

¼	tsp	sugar	1 mL
1	tsp	salt	5 mL
¾	cup	salad or olive oil	175 mL
¼	cup	vinegar (plain, wine or herb)	50 mL
¼	cup	pickle relish	50 mL

Combine all ingredients in jar and shake. Cook vegetable (e.g. brussel sprouts, broccoli, carrots) and add 1 Tbsp (15mL) of sauce per vegetable serving.

Barley with Mushrooms

¼	cup	butter or margarine	50	mL
½	lb	mushrooms, sliced	250	g
1		large onion, chopped	1	
1	cup	pearl barley	250	mL
2		cans (10oz/284/mL) consommé	2	

Preheat oven to 350°F (180°). Sauté mushrooms and onion in butter, stir in barley and brown lightly. Add soup.
Bake in casserole for 45-60 minutes or until liquid is absorbed and barley is tender.
Serves 6.

Sesame Pilaf

¼	cup	butter or margarine	50	mL
1	cup	rice	250	mL
2	cups	boiling water	500	mL
2		chicken bouillon cubes	2	
½	tsp	salt	2	mL
1½	cup	frozen peas	375	mL
¼	cup	toasted sesame seeds	50	mL

Brown rice in butter; add next 3 ingredients and bring to a boil. Cover. Reduce heat to minimum; cook until liquid is absorbed (25-35 minutes). Add frozen peas and sesame seeds. Keep on heat until peas are hot.
Serves 6.

Casual

Eggs Royale Casserole

Great for Christmas morning!

2	cups	croutons, herb seasoned	500	mL
1	cup	shredded cheese	250	mL
4		eggs, slightly beaten	4	
2	cups	milk	500	mL
½	tsp	salt	2	mL
½	tsp	mustard	2	mL
⅛	tsp	onion powder	.5	mL
½	tsp	pepper	2	mL
10		slices bacon, cooked crisp	10	

Preheat oven to 325°F (160°C). Combine croutons and cheese; put in bottom of greased 2 qt (2L) casserole. Mix next 6 ingredients and pour over croutons and cheese. Crumble bacon on top.
Bake 55-60 minutes.
Note: May be assembled the night before and baked in the morning.
Serves 6.

Fake Caviar

1		can pitted ripe olives, chopped	1	
½	cup	green onions, chopped	125	mL
½	cup	old cheddar cheese, grated	125	mL
½	cup	mayonnaise	125	mL
½	tsp	curry powder	2	mL
½	tsp	salt (optional)	2	mL
5		English muffins	5	

Preheat oven to 350°F (180°C). Combine all ingredients and spread on 10 muffin halves.
Bake 10 minutes. Serve with salad for lunch.
Note: May be cut in bite-size pieces and served as hors d'oeuvres.
Serves 10.

Krabbenauflauf with Cheese

A German shrimp strata.

½		onion, chopped	½	
2		celery stalks, chopped	2	
2	Tbsp	oil	30	mL
2		slices of bread, cubed	2	
⅓	lb	shrimp	150	g
1	cup	grated Emmenthal cheese	250	mL
1		egg	1	
⅓	cup	milk	75	mL
		salt		
		Worcestershire sauce		

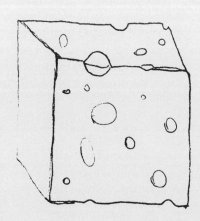

Preheat oven to 400°F (200°C). Brown onion and celery in oil in skillet or casserole. Add bread, sauté for another 5 minutes. Put half of mixture in casserole; layer in shrimp and cheese. Beat last 4 ingredients, pour over mixture in casserole.
Bake, uncovered, 25 minutes.
Serves 2-3.

Shepherd's Pie Plus

Favorite family fare.

5		slices of bacon, cut in 1" (2.5cm) pieces	5	
2		large onions, chopped	2	
1	Tbsp	oil	15	mL
1	lb	lean ground beef	500	g
3	Tbsp	flour	45	mL
2		beef bouillon cubes	2	
1		can (28oz/796mL) tomatoes, drained, reserving liquid salt, pepper to taste	1	
½	tsp	thyme	2	mL
½	tsp	cayenne pepper	2	mL
1	Tbsp	paprika	15	mL
3	Tbsp	parsley flakes	45	mL
2	cups	frozen peas	500	mL
6-8		large potatoes, cooked, mashed with salt, pepper, butter, and cream	6-8	

Preheat oven to 400°F (200°C). Prepare potatoes which will be used for topping. In a large skillet cook bacon until nearly crisp. Drain fat. To the same pan add oil and onions and cook until soft. Add ground beef and brown. Stir in flour, beef bouillon, liquid from tomatoes, salt and pepper. Cook slowly. Add thyme, cayenne and paprika. In a large shallow casserole place half of beef mixture. Cover with tomatoes, peas, and parsley. Add remaining beef mixture. Cover with prepared mashed potatoes.
Bake it for 40 minutes or until thoroughly heated.
Note: (4 to 6 garden fresh tomatoes and 1 cup of water may be substituted for canned tomatoes.)
Serves 4-6.

Meat Loaf

Great cold for picnics!

3	lbs	ground pork	1.5	kg
1		medium onion, diced	1	
1		clove garlic, minced	1	
2	Tbsp	butter or bacon fat	30	mL
1	Tbsp	salt	15	mL
1	Tbsp	paprika	15	mL
5		hard boiled eggs	5	

Preheat oven to 350°F (180°C). Melt butter in saucepan and fry onions and garlic until soft. Mix with ground pork, salt and paprika in large bowl. Using a 9x13" (22x34cm) baking dish, place a 3" (7.5cm) wide strip of meat mixture down length of pan. Place eggs down the centre and pat remainder of meat around eggs covering them completely and joining bottom layer.
Bake for approximately 1½ hours or until a bit crisp on top. Baste a few times with fat which accumulates.
Serves 8-10.

Minute Meat Loaf

1	lb	medium ground beef	500	g
1	lb	lean ground pork	500	g
1		pkg onion soup mix	1	
1		egg, beaten	1	
2	cups	sour cream	500	mL
		salt and pepper		

Preheat oven to 350°F (180°C). Mix all ingredients.
Bake for 1 hour. Serve hot or cold with favorite sauce, e.g. chili sauce, salsa, or chutney.
Serves 6.

#1 Chow Mein

Looks long but just takes minutes. Besides tasting wonderful it's a great way to use leftover chicken or turkey.

1		large onion, thinly sliced	1	
4		large stalks celery, sliced	4	
¾	lb	small, whole mushrooms	375	g
½	lb	bean sprouts	250	g
5	Tbsp	butter, divided	75	mL
½		pkg (14oz/397g) fine steam fried noodles	½	
½		pkg (14oz/397g) regular steam fried noodles	½	
2	cups	chicken in julienne strips	500	mL
1	cup	whole almonds, toasted	250	mL

Sauce

1	cup	boiling water	250	mL
1		chicken bouillon cube	1	
3	Tbsp	soy sauce	45	mL
1	Tbsp	cornstarch	15	mL
		cold water		

Sauté onion in 1 Tbsp (15mL) butter until soft. Place in a large heavy stew pot over low heat. Sauté celery in 1 Tbsp (15mL) butter for 1 minute. Add to pot. Sauté mushrooms in 2 Tbsp (30mL) butter until lightly browned. Add to pot. Sauté bean sprouts in remaining butter for 30 seconds. Add to pot. Place noodles in a large collander. Pour a kettle of boiling water through. Add to the pot along with chicken and almonds and mix thoroughly. Pour sauce over and mix again.

Sauce
In a small saucepan dissolve bouillon cube in boiling water. Add soy sauce. Mix cornstarch in a little cold water and add to sauce. Cook and stir until thickened slightly.
Serves 6.

Church Supper Tuna Bake

¾	cup	chopped green pepper	175	mL
3	cups	sliced celery	750	mL
2		medium onions, chopped	2	
¼	cup	butter	50	mL
3		cans (10oz/284mL) cream of mushroom soup	3	
1½	cups	milk	375	mL
3	cups	shredded Swiss cheese	750	mL
24	oz	medium noodles, cooked	750	g
5-6		cans (6.5oz/184g) tuna, drained	5-6	
1½	cups	mayonnaise	375	mL
¾	cup	diced pimento	175	mL
1	cup	slivered, blanched almonds, toasted	250	mL

Preheat oven to 450°F (230°C). Cook the first 4 ingredients together for 5 minutes. Blend soup and milk. Add cheese and heat, stirring until cheese melts. Combine the next 4 ingredients. Add cheese sauce and vegetables and mix. Turn into 2 greased 13x9x2" (34x22x4cm) pans. Sprinkle almonds over top.
Bake for 35 minutes or until hot and bubbly.
Note: For a creamier casserole use fewer noodles.
Serves 24.

Shrimp Casserole

A fabulous casserole - everyone's favorite!

4	cups	cooked rice, cold	1	L
¾	lb	cooked shrimp	375	g
½	cup	slivered almonds, toasted	125	mL
¾	lb	sliced mushrooms, sautéed	375	g
½	cup	chopped green onion	125	mL
1	cup	diced sharp cheddar cheese	250	mL
1½		cans (10oz/284g) cream of mushroom soup	1½	
1	Tbsp	minced fresh parsley	15	mL
¼	tsp	dill	1	mL
		salt and pepper to taste		

Preheat oven to 325°F (160°C). Combine ingredients in a 2 qt (2L) greased casserole.
Bake for approximately 40 minutes.
Note: This is also excellent with cubed chicken and is a wonderful way to use leftover turkey.
Serves 6.

Pot Roast with Noodles

This is a shortcut version which makes a creamy, rich, mushroom sauce, without any work in last minute thickening.

3	lb	boneless rump roast	1.5 k
		rosemary	
		thyme	
1		clove garlic, minced	1
		seasoning salt	
		freshly ground pepper	
		flour	
¼	cup	oil	50 mL
2	Tbsp	instant minced onion	30 mL
½	cup	extra dry vermouth (or dry white or red wine)	125 mL
1		can (10oz/284mL) cream of mushroom soup	1
½		soup can water	½
12		large fresh mushrooms	12
		paprika	
12-14		small whole carrots	12-14
		fresh parsley, chopped	

Preheat oven to 300°F (150°C). Rub meat generously with spices and dredge in flour. Heat oil in dutch oven, and brown meat on all sides. Add next 5 ingredients. Sprinkle with paprika.
Bake for 3 hours. Turn meat, stirring sauce and basting once during cooking. Add carrots and continue cooking ½ hour longer. Serve with broad noodles and lots of fresh chopped parsley on each serving.
Note: A boneless shoulder roast, well trimmed, rolled, and tied also makes a delicious pot roast. A can of button mushrooms, with liquid can be substituted for fresh mushrooms. In this case eliminate the ½ soup can of water. Also try subsituting 2 lb (1kg) lean stewing beef or cut up round steak for the pot roast.
Serves 6.

Cheese and Meat Casserole

1	Tbsp	oil	15 mL
1		large onion, chopped	1
1		can (10oz/284mL) mushrooms, drained	1
2	lbs	lean ground beef	1 k
3		cans (10oz/284mL) meatless Chef Boyardee sauce	3
		salt and pepper to taste	
1		pkg (12oz/375g) fine egg noodles, cooked	1
1	lb	sharp cheese, grated	500 g

Preheat oven to 350°F (180°C). Brown onions in oil in a large skillet. Add mushrooms and meat and cook until meat browns. Add sauce, salt and pepper and simmer for 5 minutes. In 2 casseroles (one large and one small) layer as follows: noodles, sauce, cheese. Repeat. Top with cheese.
Bake for 1 hour.
Serves 10-12.

Crab Supper Pie

A cousin of the famous quiche.

1		unbaked 9" (23cm) pie shell	1
1	cup	shredded Swiss cheese	250 mL
1	cup	crabmeat	250 mL
2		green onions, sliced	2
3		eggs, beaten	3
1	cup	light cream	250 mL
½	tsp	salt	2 mL
½	tsp	grated lemon peel	2 mL
¼	tsp	dry mustard	1 mL
		pinch of mace	
¼	cup	sliced almonds	50 mL

Preheat oven to 325°F (160°C). Sprinkle cheese, crab and onion in layers in pie shell. Combine the next 6 ingredients and pour into pie shell. Top with almonds.
Bake 45 minutes or until set. Remove from oven and let stand 10 minutes before serving.
Serves 6.

Crescent Italiano Bake

1	lb	ground beef	500 g
1	cup	chopped mushrooms	250 mL
½	cup	chopped onion	125 mL
½	tsp	each, salt and pepper	2 mL
1		can (7½oz/227mL) tomato sauce	1
1	cup	grated cheddar cheese	250 mL
½	cup	sour cream	125 mL
¼	tsp	oregano	1 mL
¼	tsp	rosemary or basil	1 mL
1		can (8oz/227g) refrigerator crescent rolls	1

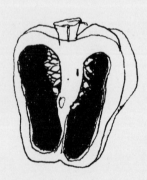

Preheat oven to 375°F (190°C). In a skillet, brown the first 3 ingredients. Add seasonings and tomato sauce. Pour mixture into ungreased 8x12" (21x30cm) baking dish and sprinkle with cheese. Combine the next 3 ingredients. Set aside. Separate crescent dough into 8 triangles; spread with sour cream mixture. Roll up, starting at wide end; arrange on top of casserole.
Bake 25-30 minutes, or until golden brown.
Serves 4-6.

Chicken Parmesan

1	cup	dry breadcrumbs	250	mL
½	cup	grated parmesan cheese	125	mL
3	Tbsp	finely chopped parsley	45	mL
¾	tsp	salt	3	mL
1	tsp	dry mustard	5	mL
½	tsp	Worcestershire sauce	2	mL
½	cup	butter, melted	125	mL
1		large broiler-fryer (3lbs/1.5kg) cut into serving pieces	1	

Preheat oven to 350°F (180°C). In shallow pan, combine first 4 ingredients. In separate bowl blend next 3 ingredients. Dip chicken in butter mixture and then crumb mixture. Place in large shallow pan. Bake for 45-60 minutes.
Serves 4.

Chicken "McNugs"

1	cup	fine cracker crumbs	250	mL
¼	cup	ground almonds or sesame seeds	50	mL
¼	cup	grated parmesan cheese	50	mL
½	tsp	garlic powder	2	mL
		seasoning salt, pepper to taste		
		melted butter		
3		chicken breasts, halved, boned and cut into cubes	3	

Preheat oven to 400°F (200°C). Combine first 6 ingredients in a shallow bowl. Dip chicken cubes into melted butter and then crumb mixture.
Bake for 15 minutes.
Note: These McNugs may be frozen after cooking.
Serves a crowd.

Cheesy Spinach Lasagne

9		lasagne noodles, cooked	9	
1		pkg (10oz/300g) frozen chopped spinach, thawed and drained	1	
4		large eggs, lightly beaten	4	
1	lb	ricotta or cottage cheese	500	g
1	tsp	salt	5	mL
		pepper to taste		
2	tsp	butter	10	mL
¼	cup	chopped onion	50	mL
2		garlic cloves, minced	2	
12	oz	grated mozzarella cheese	375	g

Sauce

¼	cup	butter	50	mL
¼	cup	flour	50	mL
2	cups	milk or half and half cream	500	mL
¾-1	cup	grated parmesan cheese	175-250	mL
		salt, pepper to taste		

Preheat oven to 350°F (180°C). Combine spinach with next 4 ingredients. Sauté onion and garlic in butter until golden and add spinach mixture. Arrange three lasagne strips lengthwise over bottom of greased 13x9" (34x22cm) pan. Cover with half of spinach mixture and mozzarella cheese. Repeat layers. Top with remaining three strips of lasagne. Prepare sauce by blending butter and flour over low heat. Stir in milk gradually. Add ½ - ¾ cup (125-175mL) parmesan cheese and heat, stirring constantly until thickened. Season. Pour over lasagne. Sprinkle with remaining parmesan.
Bake for 35 minutes.
Serves 8.

Sole Au Vin Blanc

8		fillets of sole	8
		seasonings of your choice	
¾	cup	white wine	175 mL
2	Tbsp	butter	30 mL
2	Tbsp	flour	30 mL
½	cup	cream	125 mL
		parsley	
		breadcrumbs	
		butter	

Preheat oven to 350°F (180°C). Roll fillets and place in baking dish. Add seasonings and wine. Cover and bake 15 minutes. Make sauce of butter, flour, and cream, pour wine from cooked sole into sauce; stir 3-4 minutes. Pour sauce over fillets; sprinkle with parsley and crumbs; dot with butter.
Brown delicately under broiler.
Serves 4.

Tuna in Shells

Super and quick!

2	cans (6.5oz/184g) tuna	2
	mayonnaise	
	dash Worcestershire sauce	
4	patty shells	4
	bread or cracker crumbs	
	warm sherry	

Preheat oven to 350°F (180°C). Mix tuna with enough mayonnaise to make it creamy; add few drops of Worcestershire sauce. Fill patty shells; sprinkle with crumbs.
Heat in oven; serve with warm sherry to pour over.
Serves 4.

Barbequed Pork Chops

6		pork chops	6
½	tsp	salt	2 mL
⅛	tsp	pepper	.5 mL
1	cup	chili sauce	250 mL
½	cup	water	125 mL
¼	cup	vinegar	50 mL
2	Tbsp	brown sugar	30 mL
1	Tbsp	chopped onion	15 mL
1	tsp	dry mustard	5 mL
1	tsp	Worcestershire sauce	5 mL

Preheat oven to 325°F (160°C). Season chops and place in uncovered casserole. Make sauce of remaining ingredients and pour over chops. Bake ½ hour. Turn chops; skim off fat; baste with sauce and bake until tender 1-1½ hours.
Serves 4-6.

Spareribs - Easy and Delicious

3-4	lb	pork spareribs	1.5-2 kg
		hickory smoked salt	
¼	cup	honey	50 mL
¼	cup	soy sauce	50 mL
¼	cup	lime juice	50 mL
½	cup	ketchup	125 mL

Preheat oven to 350°F (180°C). Cut the ribs in serving pieces and sprinkle with the salt.
Bake for 45 minutes. Pour off excess fat. Mix remaining ingredients and pour over ribs and continue to bake for an additional 30 minutes, basting frequently.
Serves 4.

Sweet and Sauer Burger

1		pkg onion soup mix	1
¼	cup	water	50 mL
1		egg, beaten	1
1½	lb	ground beef	750 g
1	cup	sauerkraut, drained	250 mL
½	cup	whole berry cranberry sauce	125 mL
¼	cup	water	50 mL
3	Tbsp	brown sugar	45 mL
6		enriched onion rolls	6

Combine the first 3 ingredients; let stand for 5 minutes. Add beef and mix thoroughly. Shape into 6 patties. Combine the next 4 ingredients in a saucepan; simmer for 20 minutes. Serve as hamburgers on buns with a dollop of sauce on each pattie or as an entrée with sauce, accompanied by hot buttered noodles and dill pickles.
Makes 6 patties.

Liver and Bacon

1½	lbs	calves' liver, sliced	750 g
¼	cup	flour	50 mL
2	tsp	paprika	10 mL
½	lb	bacon	250 g
2		apples, peeled and sliced	2
1		onion cut in wedges	1

Dredge liver in flour and paprika mixture and cook in butter until tender. Use another pan to cook bacon until crisp. Drain off some of the fat and sauté the onions and apples. To serve, spoon bacon mixture on top of liver slices.
Note: Herbed mashed potatoes, i.e. mashed potatoes mixed with egg, chopped parsley, dill, basil or whatever is in season, would be nice with this dish.
Serves 4-6.

Meatballs

These have a lovely soft texture because of the veal and pork. Try them with your favorite sauce, and you won't make any others!

¾	lb	lean ground beef	375	g
¼	lb	ground pork	125	g
¼	lb	ground veal	125	g
½	tsp	savory	2	mL
½	tsp	marjoram	2	mL
2		eggs, beaten lightly	2	
1		clove garlic, minced	1	
2	Tbsp	chopped fresh parsley	30	mL
½	cup	grated sharp cheddar cheese	125	mL

Mix all ingredients together stirring gently with a fork. Shape into large balls, golfball size. (These will not be firm and round.) Lightly brown in oil and add to your sauce for the last 15-20 minutes.
Note: Equally good with meatloaf mixture of equal portions of beef, pork, veal.
Serves 4.

Tourtière

A Quebec Christmas tradition which goes back hundreds of years. In our house, it is annual Christmas Eve fare.

1	lb	minced pork	500 g
1		small onion, chopped	1
1		garlic clove, minced	1
½	tsp	salt	2 mL
¼	tsp	celery salt	1 mL
¼	tsp	ground cloves	1 mL
½	tsp	cinnamon	2 mL
½	tsp	savory	2 mL
½	cup	water	125 mL
¼-½		breadcrumbs	50-125 mL
		pastry for 2 crust pie	

Preheat oven to 400°F (200°C). Place all ingredients except breadcrumbs in saucepan; bring to a boil and cook, uncovered, for 20 minutes. Remove from heat and stir in half the breadcrumbs. Let stand for 10 minutes. If fat is sufficiently absorbed by crumbs, add no more, if not, continue in same manner. When cool, pour into pastry lined pie plate; cover with crust.
Bake about ½ hour or until golden brown. Serve with cinnamon applesauce or maple syrup, and baked beans on the side.
Note: A baked tourtière may be stored 4-5 months in freezer.
Serves 6-8.

Nasi Goreng

2	cups	long-grain rice	500	mL
2	cups	chicken bouillon	500	mL
4	cups	water	1	L
		salt to taste, dab butter		
1	Tbsp	cooking oil	15	mL
1		large onion, chopped	1	
2		celery stalks, chopped	2	
3		cloves garlic, chopped	3	
½	tsp	grated fresh ginger root	2	mL
1	Tbsp	sambal oelek (hot pepper sauce or 4 hot red peppers)	15	mL
2	tsp	curry	10	mL
1	Tbsp	kecap manis (sweet soy sauce)	15	mL
2		green peppers, diced	2	
1½	cups	shredded cabbage	375	mL
3		carrots, diced or julienned	3	
2	cups	diced, cooled chicken, turkey, ham, pork or a combination of same	500	mL
1	cup	shrimp	250	mL

Cook rice until slightly underdone. In a large heavy saucepan or wok (the wok is best) heat oil and sauté onion until soft always stirring. Add next 6 ingredients and sauté two minutes. Add next 3 ingredients and sauté three minutes. Add shrimp and chicken or pork and sauté two minutes. Add rice and sauté until lightly brown. Adjust seasonings perhaps increasing sambal oelek and kecap manis.
Serves 12.

Breads

Pumpkin Loaf

A moist, nutritious loaf that keeps well if it lasts long enough.

1	cup	oil	250 mL
1 ½	cups	liquid honey	375 mL
2	cups	canned pumpkin	500 mL
2		eggs, slightly beaten	2
3	cups	whole wheat flour	750 mL
½	cup	bran or wheat germ	125 mL
2	tsp	baking powder	10 mL
1	tsp	salt	5 mL
1	tsp	baking soda	5 mL
1	tsp	cinnamon	5 mL
1	tsp	nutmeg	5 mL
2	cups	raisins, dates or combination	500 mL
1	cup	chopped walnuts	250 mL

Preheat oven to 350 °F(180°C). Mix together the first 4 ingredients. Stir together the next 7 ingredients and add to the first mixture, mixing thoroughly. Stir in fruit and nuts. Spoon into a greased and floured 10" (3L) tube pan.
Bake for 1½ hours. Cool in pan.
Serves a crowd.

Apricot Bread

1½	cups	dried apricots, chopped	375 mL
1	cup	boiling water	250 mL
½	tsp	baking soda	2 mL
1	cup	sugar	250 mL
2		large eggs	2
2¾	cups	flour	675 mL
1	Tbsp	baking powder	15 mL
1	cup	chopped nuts	250 mL

Preheat oven to 350°F (180°C). Pour boiling water over apricots and soak until just tender. Drain water into a cup and add more , if necessary, to make 1 cup (250mL). Pour liquid into mixing bowl; add remaining ingredients, blending well. Divide batter into two loaf pans. Bake about 45 minutes or until straw comes out of centre clean. Makes 2 loaves.

Tasty Fruit Loaf

2	cups	flour	500 mL
1	cup	sugar	250 mL
1½	tsp	baking powder	7 mL
1	tsp	salt	5 mL
½	cup	soft shortening	125 mL
½	cup	milk	125 mL
1	tsp	vanilla	5 mL
2		eggs	2
1½	cups	fruit (glazed cherries, nuts, raisins, currants, peel or what's on hand)	375 mL

Preheat oven to 350°F(180°C). Sift first 4 ingredients. Add next 3 ingredients and beat 2 minutes. Add eggs and beat 2 minutes. Fold in the fruit . Spoon into a greased loaf pan.
Bake for 1 to 1¼ hours. Freezes well.
Makes 1 loaf.

English Muffins In A Loaf

Relatively fast - no kneading, 1 rising.

5½-6	cups	flour, divided	1375-1500	mL
2		pkgs active dry yeast	2	
1	Tbsp	sugar	15	mL
2	tsp	salt	10	mL
¼	tsp	baking soda	1	mL
2	cups	milk	500	mL
½	cup	water	125	mL
		cornmeal		

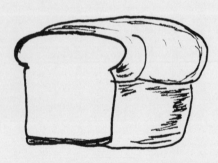

Preheat oven to 400°F(200°C). Grease 2 loaf pans, sprinkle with cornmeal. Combine three cups flour (750mL) with next 4 ingredients. Heat liquids until hot, not boiling and add to dry mixture. Beat well. Stir in enough remaining flour to make a stiff batter. Spoon into pans; sprinkle tops with cornmeal. Cover; let rise in warm place 45 minutes.
Bake 25 minutes; remove from pan immediately to cool.
Makes 2 loaves.

Take One French Loaf...

Mozzarella Bread

⅔	cup	butter, softened	150 mL
1	tsp	oregano	5 mL
1	tsp	garlic powder	5 mL
½	cup	grated parmesan cheese	125 mL
1		loaf unsliced French bread	1
8	oz	mozzarella cheese slices	250 g

Preheat oven to 425°F (220°C). Mix first 4 ingredients together. Slice loaf in half lengthwise. Spread each half with the butter mixture. Top with cheese slices, covering completely.
Bake for 10 minutes. Slice in 2" pieces.

French Onion Bread

2		loaves French bread	2
1	cup	softened butter	250 mL
1		pkg (1½oz/42g) onion soup mix	1

Preheat oven to 350°F (180°C). Split loaves in half lengthwise; cream the soup mix and butter and spread on cut sides. Place sides together. Wrap in foil.
Bake for 20 minutes.

Onion-Sourcream Bread

1		loaf French bread	1
1		tin French fried onion rings	1
½	cup	butter, melted	125 mL
1	cup	sour cream	250 mL

Preheat oven to 350°F (180°C). Cut bread in 1½" (4cm) thick slices. Place onions in a bowl and crush slightly. Mix butter and sour cream. Dip slices into sour cream mixture and then into crushed onions. Place on baking sheet.
Bake 20 minutes or until crusty brown.

Toasted Herb Rolls in a Loaf

Yummy!

1		loaf unsliced white bread	1	
1	cup	butter or margarine	250	mL
½	tsp	thyme	2	mL
¼	tsp	salt	1	mL
¼	tsp	paprika	1	mL
¼	tsp	dried savory or poultry seasoning	1	mL

Preheat oven to 375°F (190°C). Remove all crusts from bread except bottom one. Cut loaf in half horizontally. Then slice vertically, to bottom crust (or through it), every 2" (5cm). Blend butter and seasonings; spread between cuts, over tops, sides and ends.
Bake uncovered for 20 minutes.
Note: May be prepared ahead. Freeze or refrigerate.
Serves 8-10.

Easy Cheese Bread

Excellent toasted.

2½	cups	packaged biscuit mix	625	mL
1	cup	shredded sharp cheese	250	mL
2	tsp	poppy seeds	10	mL
1		egg, beaten	1	
1	cup	milk	250	mL

Preheat oven to 350°F (180°C). Mix dry ingredients. Beat egg in milk; add to dry mixture. Stir until just moistened. Spoon into greased loaf pan.
Bake 45-50 minutes.
Makes 1 loaf.

Mexican Corn Bread

A southern staple with added spice!

1¼	cups	cornmeal	300	mL
½	cup	flour	125	mL
1	Tbsp	baking powder	15	mL
1	tsp	salt	5	mL
2		eggs	2	
1¼	cups	milk	300	mL
¾	cup	grated sharp cheddar cheese	175	mL
½	cup	vegetable oil	125	mL
½	cup	canned cream-style corn	125	mL
1		medium onion, minced	1	
3	Tbsp	bacon bits	45	mL
2	Tbsp	finely chopped jalapeno peppers	30	mL

Preheat oven to 350°F (180°C). Butter 10" (25cm) iron skillet; place in oven until hot. Mix first 4 ingredients. Mix remaining ingredients; add to dry mixture and stir just until blended. Spoon into skillet.
Bake 30 minutes or until toothpick inserted into centre comes out clean. Note: Spiciness may be regulated by increasing or decreasing the amount of peppers. For extra Mexican touch, serve with salsa sauce. Serves 12.

Special Pineapple Carrot Muffins

Moist and flavorful with a surprise ingredient.

2	cups	flour	500 mL
1	tsp	soda	5 mL
2	tsp	cinnamon	10 mL
1	tsp	salt	5 mL
2	cups	sugar	500 mL
1	cup	oil	250 mL
3		eggs	3
2	cups	finely grated carrot	500 mL
1	cup	well drained crushed pineapple	250 mL
1	cup	coconut	250 mL
1	cup	chopped walnuts	250 mL
1	tsp	vanilla	5 mL

Preheat oven to 350°F (180°C). Sift together the first 4 ingredients and set aside. Combine the next 3 and beat well. Gradually add the flour mixture. Add remaining ingredients, mixing thoroughly. Spoon into greased muffin pans.
Bake for 20 - 25 minutes.
Variations: Batter may be baked in bundt or loaf pans. Increase baking time to 1 hour.
Makes 24 large muffins.

Banana Chocolate Chip Muffins

For those who can't live without chocolate!

1	cup	mashed bananas	250 mL
¾	cup	sugar	175 mL
1		egg, slightly beaten	1
⅓	cup	margarine, melted	75 mL
1½	cups	flour	375 mL
1	tsp	baking powder	5 mL
1	tsp	baking soda	5 mL
½	tsp	salt	2 mL
¼	cup	chocolate chips	50 mL

Preheat oven to 375°F (190°C). Combine the first 3 ingredients, mix in the margarine. Combine the dry ingredients and stir into banana mixture until blended. Stir in the chocolate chips. Fill muffin cups ⅔ full.
Bake for 20 minutes or until cooked.
Makes 12 muffins.

Blueberry Yogurt Muffins

"Miss Nutritious Muffin"-Winner of the 4th annual nutritious muffin contest at the University Hill Secondary School.

2	cups	plain yogurt	500	mL
2	tsp	baking soda	10	mL
1	cup	brown sugar	250	mL
2		eggs	2	
1	cup	sunflower oil	250	mL
2	cups	wheat germ (bran may be subsituted)	500	mL
1	Tbsp	vanilla	15	mL
2	cups	whole wheat flour	500	mL
1⅓	Tbsp	baking powder	20	mL
½	tsp	salt	2	mL
2	cups	blueberries	500	mL

Preheat oven to 350°F (180°C). Mix yogurt and baking soda together. In a large bowl, combine sugar, eggs and oil. Blend in wheat germ and vanilla. Set aside. Sift flour, baking powder and salt. Add to sugar mixture alternately with yogurt mixture. Fold in blueberries. Fill 24 medium size greased muffin tins.
Bake for 20-25 minutes.
Makes 24 muffins.

Sunshine Orange Muffins

1		whole orange, unpeeled, cut in pieces	1	
½	cup	orange juice	125	mL
1		egg	1	
½	cup	oil	125	mL
½	cup	sugar	125	mL
1½	cups	flour, white or whole wheat	375	mL
1	tsp	baking soda	5	mL
1	tsp	baking powder	5	mL
½	cup	raisins or chopped dates	125	mL
½	cup	chopped walnuts	125	mL

Preheat oven to 375°F (190°C). In a blender combine orange and juice and blend. Add egg, oil and sugar and blend well. Stir together the remaining ingredients. Pour blender mixture over and combine. Spoon into greased muffin pan.
Bake 15-20 minutes.
Makes 12 large muffins.

Wheat Germ Muffins

1	cup	whole wheat flour	250	mL
1	Tbsp	baking powder	15	mL
⅛	tsp	baking soda	.5	mL
¾	cup	wheat germ	175	mL
¼	cup	brown sugar	50	mL
¾	cup	milk	175	mL
¼	cup	salad oil	50	mL
1		egg	1	
1-1½	cups	raisins	250-375	mL

Preheat oven to 400°F (200°C). Mix dry ingredients. Make a well and mix in "wet" ingredients. Add raisins. Spoon into prepared muffin pan.
Bake for 10-12 minutes.
Makes 10 large or 12 small muffins.

Fresh Fruit Coffee Cake

Nice freshly baked, but also freezes well.

½	cup	butter or margarine	125 mL
½	cup	sugar	125 mL
2		eggs, well beaten	2
		grated rind of small lemon	
⅔	cup	flour	150 mL
½	cup	potato or rice flour	125 mL
1	tsp	baking powder	5 mL
		any fresh fruit, eg. sliced apples, berries, peaches, plums etc.	

Preheat oven to 325°F (160°C). Cream butter and sugar. Add eggs and lemon rind, beating well. Add sifted dry ingredients, mixing to blend. Spread into a greased 9" (22 cm) square cake pan. Lightly press fresh fruit all over top to cover completely.
Bake 40-45 minutes.
Serves 8-10.

Chocolate Coffee Cake

1	cup	butter, softened	250 mL
1½	cups	sugar	375 mL
4		eggs	4
3	cups	flour	750 mL
1	Tbsp	baking powder	15 mL
1	tsp	baking soda	5 mL
		pinch of salt	
1½	cups	sour cream	375 mL
1	cup	chocolate syrup	250 mL
1	tsp	cinnamon	5 mL

Preheat oven to 350°F (180°C). Grease and flour a 10" (3L) tube pan. Cream butter and sugar; add eggs one at a a time, beating well. Sift dry ingredients and add alternately with sour cream, mixing well. Stir cinnamon into chocolate syrup. Alternate layers of batter and chocolate syrup in tube pan. Draw knife through batter to marble.
Bake approximately one hour.
Serves 10-12.

Poppy Seed Coffee Cake

½	cup	poppy seeds	125 mL
1	cup	buttermilk	250 mL
2	tsp	cocoa	10 mL
⅓	cup	white sugar	75 mL
1	tsp	cinnamon	5 mL
½	cup	margarine	125 mL
½	cup	shortening	125 mL
4		eggs, separated	4
1½	cups	white sugar	375 mL
2½	cups	flour	625 mL
1	tsp	baking soda	5 mL
2	tsp	baking powder	10 mL
½	tsp	salt	2 mL
1	tsp	vanilla	5 mL

Preheat oven to 350°F (180°C). Soak poppy seeds in buttermilk. Combine next 3 ingredients and set aside. Cream margarine and shortening. Add egg yolks one at a time. Combine dry ingredients. Add alternately with buttermilk mixture. Add vanilla. Beat egg whites until stiff; fold into batter. Pour ½ batter into greased (9" or 2.5L) tube pan. Sprinkle with ½ cocoa mixture. Pour in remaining batter and sprinkle top with remaining cocoa mixture.
Bake 1 hour or more. Cool in pan. Freezes well.
Serves 10-12.

Cranberry Coffee Cake

Topping

¾	cup	brown sugar	175 mL
½	cup	flour	125 mL
1	tsp	cinnamon	5 mL
¼	cup	butter or margarine	50 mL

Cake

½	cup	butter or margarine	125 mL
1	cup	white sugar	250 mL
2		eggs	1
1	tsp	vanilla	5 mL
2	cups	flour	500 mL
1	tsp	baking powder	5 mL
1	tsp	baking soda	5 mL
½	tsp	salt	2 mL
1	cup	sour cream	250 mL
2	cups	cranberries, fresh or frozen	500 mL

Preheat oven to 350°F (180°C). For streusel topping, blend first 4 ingredients until crumbly . Set aside. Cream butter and sugar. Beat in eggs one at a time. Sift dry ingredients and add alternately with sour cream to creamed mixture. In a springform pan, layer ½ batter, ½ streusel, ½ cranberries. Repeat.
Bake for 45 - 60 minutes. Serve with whipped cream.
Serves a crowd.

Marble Coffee Cake

3		eggs, well beaten	3	
½	cup	butter or margarine	125	mL
1	cup	sugar	250	mL
1	tsp	vanilla	5	mL
1¾	cup	flour	425	mL
1½	tsp	baking powder	7	mL
1	tsp	baking soda	5	mL
1	cup	sour cream	250	mL
¾	cup	brown sugar	175	mL
2	tsp	cinnamon	10	mL

Preheat oven to 350°F (180°C). Cream butter and sugar. Add eggs and vanilla. Mix dry ingredients and fold in, combining well. Fold in sour cream. Sprinkle brown sugar and cinnamon over batter and swirl with a knife to marble. Pour into a greased springform pan.
Bake for 55 minutes.
Makes 1 large coffee cake.

Wheaten Bread

Wholesome, hale & hearty!

4	cups	graham flour	1000	mL
1	cup	wheat germ	250	mL
1	cup	whole wheat flour	250	mL
1	cup	white flour	250	mL
¼	cup	sugar	50	mL
1⅓	Tbsp	baking soda	20	mL
1	Tbsp	salt	15	mL
4	cups	buttermilk	1000	mL

Preheat oven to 350°F (180°C). Mix dry ingredients. Add buttermilk and blend well. Spoon into 2 greased loaf pans.
Bake for 1 hour.
Makes 2 loaves.

Desserts

Apple Cheesecake Tarte

Fabulous!

Crust
1	cup	all purpose flour	250 mL
½	cup	butter	125 mL
⅓	cup	sugar	75 mL
¼	tsp	vanilla	1 mL

Filling
1		pkg (8oz/250g) cream cheese	1
¼	cup	sugar	50 mL
1		egg	1
½	tsp	vanilla	2 mL

Topping
⅓	cup	sugar	75 mL
2-3		apples, peeled and sliced	2-3
¾	tsp	cinnamon	3 mL
½	cup	sliced almonds	125 mL

Crust
Preheat oven to 450°F (230°C). Cream butter, sugar, vanilla, blend in flour. Spread dough on sides and bottom of 9" (1L) springform pan or tart pan.

Filling
Combine filling ingredients beating until smooth. Pour into crust.

Topping
Combine sugar and cinnamon, toss with apple slices. Arrange over cream cheese. Top with almonds.

Bake for 10 minutes. Reduce heat to 400°F (200° C) and continue baking for 25 minutes or until apples are cooked. Check often so it doesn't burn. Cool. Remove sides of pan to serve.
Serves 8 - 10.

Rotegrütze

A cool, refreshing dessert for a hot summer day.

2	lb	assorted fruit, select 3 or 4 in equal amounts from blackberries or raspberries, strawberries, cherries, apricots, nectarines or peaches; be sure to include either blackberries or raspberries	1 kg
½	cup	water	125 mL
½	cup	sugar	125 mL
½	cup	dry red wine	125 mL
2	Tbsp	cornstarch	30 mL
¼	cup	toasted slivered almonds, optional	50 mL

Combine fruit, water and sugar in a large saucepan and bring to a boil. Mix cornstarch with red wine. Take fruit off heat and add cornstarch mixture. Return to heat and cook 2 minutes, stirring until thickened. Add nuts. Cool. Turn into glass bowl and refrigerate several hours. Serve with pouring cream or whipped cream.
Serves 8 - 10.

Fruit Kabobs

bite size pieces of fruit: apples, peaches pears, banana, orange, pineapple, etc.

Marinade

2	Tbsp	honey	30 mL
2	Tbsp	orange juice	30 mL
1	tsp	cinnamon	5 mL

Alternate pieces of fruit on skewers. Baste with marinade. Grill on barbeque for 10 minutes, turning frequently.
Marinade for 4 skewers.

Chocolate Rum Pie

1		9" (22 cm) baked pastry shell or chocolate shell	1
½	cup	sugar	125 mL
1		envelope gelatin	1
		dash salt	
1	cup	milk	250 mL
2		egg yolks, beaten	2
1		pkg (6 oz/170 g) semi-sweet chocolate chips	1
½	cup	rum	125 mL
2		egg whites, beaten	2
¼	cup	sugar	50 mL
1	cup	whipping cream, whipped	250 mL
1	tsp	vanilla	5 mL

In heavy saucepan combine sugar and next 4 ingredients. Cook and stir until slightly thickened. Remove from heat, add chocolate chips, stirring until melted. Add rum and chill until partially set. Beat egg whites until soft peaks form. Gradually add sugar, beating until stiff peaks form. Fold into chocolate mixture. Garnish with whipped cream flavored with vanilla.
Serves 8.

Gâteau au Rhum

1	cup	chopped pecans	250 mL
1		golden cake mix, 2 layer size	1
4		eggs	4
½	cup	water	125 mL
½	cup	corn syrup	125 mL
½	cup	rum	125 mL
1		lemon instant pudding - 3 ¾oz size	1
¼	cup	butter	50 mL
⅛	cup	water	25 mL
1	cup	brown sugar	250 mL
½	cup	rum	125 mL

Preheat oven to 325° F (160°C). Grease a 10 " (1L) tube pan and dust with flour. Sprinkle ⅔ of nuts on bottom of pan. Beat the next 6 ingredients together to make batter; pour into pan. Sprinkle remaining nuts on top pushing gently into batter.
Bake 45 - 50 minutes.
Bring butter, water and sugar to a boil. Remove from heat and add rum. Make deep slits with a sharp knife all over cake as soon as it is removed from oven. Pour hot sauce over. Let cool completely in pan.
Serves 10 - 12.

Fresh Fruit Tart

		pastry for a 2 crust pie	
⅔	cup	grated sharp cheddar cheese	150 mL
1	cup	sugar	250 mL
½	tsp	salt	2 mL
2	Tbsp	cornstarch	30 mL
1	cup	orange juice	250 mL
¼	cup	lemon juice	50 mL
¾	cup	water	175 mL
½	tsp	each, grated orange and lemon rind	2 mL
2	cups	fresh strawberries halved (save 7 whole)	500 mL
3		fresh peaches or nectarines	3
1		banana, sliced	1
½	cup	seedless grapes	125 mL
2		kiwi fruit, sliced	2
1	cup	melon balls	250 mL
½	cup	blueberries	125 mL
2	Tbsp	sugar	30 mL
		sweetened whipped cream	

Preheat oven to 475°F (240°C). Roll dough, with cheese added, into a 15″ (38 cm) circle. Place in a large tart (flan) pan or springform pan. Prick bottom and bake 8 - 10 minutes. Cool.
To make clear orange sauce, mix dry ingredients in saucepan, gradually stirring in liquids. Bring to a boil and stir 1 minute. Remove from heat and add rind. Cool. Arrange fruit in circles with whole strawberries in centre. Sprinkle blueberries over all. Sprinkle fruit with sugar; pour over some of the sauce to glaze. Serve with whipped cream and the remaining sauce. Cointreau or other liqueur may be added to cream. Serves 8 - 10.

B.J.'s Bananas

No, she's not!

4-6		bananas	4-6
½	cup	brown sugar	125 mL
2	Tbsp	heavy cream	30 mL
1½	Tbsp	butter	22 mL
½	cup	chopped walnuts	125 mL
		whipped cream	

Allow 1 banana per serving. Peel and slice thinly into serving dishes. Make a sauce out of the next 3 ingredients. Cook slowly stirring, for 4 minutes or until sugar is melted and bubbly. Sprinkle chopped nuts on top of bananas. Pour hot sauce over. Serve with generous dollop of whipped cream.
Serves 4 - 6.

Prunes, Alice B. Toklas

48		large prunes, pitted	48
1		bottle (26oz/750mL) port	1
1	cup	sugar	250 mL
2	cups	cream, whipped	500 mL

Soak prunes in port to more than cover for 24 hours (reserve 1 cup/250mL for later). Add 1 cup/250mL more port, plus sugar. Place in saucepan; bring to a boil; boil for 1 minute. Allow prunes to cool in liquid. Refrigerate for 24-36 hours. Serve with whipped cream.
Serves 12.

Blueberry Kuchen

1	cup	flour	250 mL
⅛	tsp	salt	.5 mL
2	Tbsp	sugar	30 mL
½	cup	butter or margarine	125 mL
1	Tbsp	white vinegar	15 mL
3	cups	blueberries	750 mL
2	Tbsp	flour	30 mL
⅔	cup	sugar	150 mL
⅛	tsp	cinnamon	.5 mL
2	cups	blueberries	500 mL

Preheat oven to 400°F (200°C). Mix first 3 ingredients in blender or processor; cut in butter until mixture resembles coarse crumbs. Sprinkle with vinegar. Press into 9" (2.5L) springform pan. Make sure crust goes up sides 1¼" (16cm). Pour in 3 cups berries. Mix next 3 ingredients; sprinkle over berries.
Bake 50-60 minutes until crust is brown and filling bubbles. Remove from oven and immediately pour in 2 cups of berries. These will settle into cooked berries. Cool. Serve with ice cream or whipped cream.
Note: 3 cups frozen berries may be used but at least 2 cups should be fresh.
Serves 6-8.

Angel Mousse

4		eggs separated	4 mL
¾	cup	sugar	175 mL
¼	cup	rum	50 mL
1	tsp	vanilla	5 mL
1		envelope unflavoured gelatin	1
¼	cup	cold water	50 mL
1	cup	whipping cream, whipped	250 mL
		shaved chocolate	

Beat egg yolks and sugar until lemon coloured, add rum and vanilla. Soften gelatin in cold water for 5 minutes, dissolve over hot water until liquid. Stir into egg yolk mixture. Fold in stiffly beaten egg whites and whipped cream. Pour into dessert glasses and chill several hours. Sprinkle with shaved chocolate.
Serves 4-6.

Dessert Cheese Ball

Wonderful!

½	lb	Edam cheese, shredded	250 g
½	lb	Monterrey Jack, shredded	250 g
½	lb	pineapple cream cheese	250 g
¼	cup	golden raisins, chopped	50 mL
¼	cup	chopped nuts	50 mL
¼	cup	finely minced onion	50 mL
½	tsp	salt	2 mL
¼	tsp	white pepper	1 mL
½	cup	chopped dried mixed fruit	125 mL
1	cup	water	250 mL
½	cup	chopped nuts	250 mL

Combine the first 8 ingredients in a food processor. Soak dried fruit in water for 1 hour. Drain and blend with cheese. Roll in chopped nuts. Wrap and refrigerate at least overnight.
Makes 2 grapefruit sized balls.

Raspberry Ribbon Pie

1		9" (22cm) baked and cooled pie shell	1
Red Layer			
1		pkg (3oz/85g) raspberry gelatin	1
¼	cup	white sugar	50 mL
¼	cup	boiling water	50 mL
1		pkg (10oz/300g) frozen raspberries	1
1	Tbsp	lemon juice	15 mL
White Layer			
1	cup	cream cheese, softened	250 mL
⅓	cup	sifted icing sugar	75 mL
1	tsp	vanilla	5 mL
		dash salt	
1	cup	whipping cream, whipped, divided	250 mL

Red Layer
Dissolve gelatin and white sugar in boiling water. Add berries and lemon juice, stirring until berries are thawed. Chill until partially set.

White Layer
Blend cream cheese, icing sugar and fold in ¼ cup whipped cream. Spread half white layer on pie shell; cover with half red layer. Repeat. Chill until set. Cover with whipped cream.
Serves 8.

German Cheesecake

A wonderfully different cheesecake!

Pastry

1½	cups	flour	375 mL
1	tsp	baking powder	5 mL
½	cup	butter	125 mL
¼	cup	sugar	50 mL
1		egg	1 mL

Filling

½	cup	ground almonds	125 mL
2		cans pitted sour cherries, drained	2
1½	lbs	ricotta cheese	750 g
1	cup	sugar	250 mL
¼	cup	flour	50 mL
1	tsp	vanilla	5 mL
1	tsp	grated lemon rind	5 mL
2	Tbsp	lemon juice	30 mL
3		eggs	3
⅓	cup	melted butter, cooled	75 mL
1		egg yolk	1
1	Tbsp	water	15 mL

Preheat oven to 400°F (200°C). Mix pastry ingredients by hand. Refrigerate if soft. Pat half into a 9" (22 cm) springform pan. Sprinkle almonds over pastry. Put drained cherries over almonds. Combine the next 8 ingredients and beat until smooth. Pour over cherries. Roll remaining half of pastry. Cut into strips and criss-cross over the top.
Bake for 50 minutes. Brush with egg yolk and water mixture.
Bake 10 minutes more or until it looks cooked.
Serves 8-10.

Decadent Chocolate Mint Pie

1¼	cups	chocolate wafer crumbs	300 mL
⅓	cup	butter or margarine, melted	75 mL
2		squares semi-sweet chocolate	2
1	cup	icing sugar	250 mL
½	cup	butter or margarine	125 mL
2		eggs, beaten	2
1	tsp	vanilla	5 mL
1	tsp	peppermint extract	5 mL
		whipped cream	
		chocolate curls	

To prepare crust, mix together crumbs and melted butter. Press into a 9" (22cm) pie plate.
Bake at 300°F (150°C) for 5-8 minutes. Cool.
For filling, cream butter and sugar. Melt chocolate slowly over low heat. Add to butter mixture. Add eggs and beat at high speed until fluffy. Add vanilla and peppermint. Pour into cooled shell. Refrigerate 6 to 8 hours. Garnish with whipped cream and chocolate curls.
Serves 8.

Baked Bananas

¼	cup	butter	50 mL
¼	cup	honey	50 mL
2	Tbsp	lemon juice	30 mL
		grated lemon rind	
¾	cup	wine	175 mL
		whipped cream	
		rum (optional)	
		bananas	

Preheat oven to 400°F (200°C). Combine first 5 ingredients and heat. Pour sauce over halved bananas. Cover and hold until ready to bake for dessert.
Bake 15 minutes. Top with rum flavoured whipped cream.
Enough sauce for 6 bananas.

Chocolate Cheesecake

What a way to die!

Base

1⅓	cups	chocolate wafer cookie crumbs	325 mL
⅓	cup	melted butter or margarine	75 mL
¼	cup	sugar	50 mL

Filling

2		eggs	2
1	cup	sugar	250 mL
2	cups	cream cheese	500 mL
1		pkg (7½oz/225g) chocolate chips melted	1
½	cup	sour cream	125 mL
1	tsp	vanilla	5 mL

Garnish

whipped cream, chocolate curls or whipped cream flavoured with Cointreau or other liquer

Preheat oven to 425°F (220°C) Mix ingredients for base and press into bottom of a 10" (25cm) springform pan. Bake for 5 minutes. Turn oven to 350°F (180°C).   Combine remaining ingredients and beat for 15 minutes. Spread over shell.
Bake for 35 to 40 minutes. Garnish with whipped cream and chocolate curls.
Serves 10-12.

Almond Tarte

Reminiscent of a European pastry shop.

Crust
1	cup	flour	250 mL
½	cup	soft butter	125 mL
1	Tbsp	white sugar	15 mL
		dash salt	
1	tsp	vanilla	5 mL
1½	Tbsp	water	22 mL

Filling
¾	cup	white sugar	175 mL
¾	cup	whipping cream	175 mL
1	Tbsp	Grand Marnier	15 mL
		few drops almond extract	
1	cup	sliced almonds	250 mL

Preheat oven to 400°F (200°C).
For crust combine first 4 ingredients and beat until the consistency of coarse meal. Combine vanilla and water and add. Gather pastry into a ball and press into bottom of a 9" (22cm) tart pan.
Bake for 10-15 minutes in lower third of oven. Cool.

For filling combine all ingredients except almonds. Beat with a fork until thick. Stir in almonds. Turn into crust.
Lower oven temperature to 350°F (180°C) and bake for 45 minutes or until golden. Cool and cut into wedges.
Serves 8.

Rhubarb Pie

A new twist for a springtime favourite.

Crust
1	cup	cornflake crumbs	250 mL
1	cup	flour	250 mL
¼	cup	brown sugar	50 mL
½	cup	butter, melted	125 mL
1	tsp	cinnamon	5 mL

Filling
1		medium egg, beaten	1
1	cup	sour cream	250 mL
1¼	cups	sugar	300 mL
3	Tbsp	cornstarch	45 mL
3	cups	rhubarb	750 mL

Preheat oven to 325°F (165°C). Combine ingredients for crust and press into a 10" (25cm) pie plate, reserving ½ cup (125mL) crumbs for top. Set aside.
To prepare filling, combine egg and sour cream. Add remaining ingredients mixing well. Spread over crumbs. Sprinkle remaining ½ cup (125mL) crumbs over top.
Bake 1 hour or until knife inserted in centre comes out clean. Serve warm.
Serves 8.

Chocolate Mocha Pie

A Winner! Keep one on hand in the freezer for unexpected company.

Crust

1¼	cups	chocolate wafer crumbs	300	mL
½	cup	chopped walnuts	125	mL
⅓	cup	butter, melted	75	mL

Filling

½	cup	soft butter	125	mL
¾	cup	sugar	175	mL
1		square unsweetened chocolate melted and cooled	1	
2	tsp	instant coffee	10	mL
2		eggs	2	

Topping

2	cups	whipping cream	500	mL
½	cup	icing sugar	125	mL
2	tsp	instant coffee	10	mL
		chocolate curls		

Preheat oven to 300°F (150°C). Mix together the 3 ingredients for the crust and press into a buttered 9" (22cm) pie plate.
Bake 5-8 minutes. Cool. Beat together the first 4 filling ingredients. Add eggs one at a time and beat 5 minutes after each addition. Spread over shell and refrigerate.
Combine topping ingredients and chill 1 hour. Beat until stiff. Spread over filling. Decorate with chocolate curls if desired. Refrigerate.
Note: Don't substitute margarine for butter in filling as it will not set up properly.
Serves 6-8

Mix and Match Lemon Mousse

2	cups	whipping cream	500 mL
2		cans sweetened condensed milk	2
1		can (12oz/355mL) frozen lemonade	1

Whip cream until very stiff. Fold in condensed milk and lemonade. Freeze. Allow to stand at room temperature for 1 hour before serving. Serve in stemmed glasses garnished with whipped cream. Or serve with sliced fresh fruit or berries or with a raspberry sauce.
Serves 8-10.

Variations

Filled Meringue Shells
Spoon mousse into 2 large or several individual meringue shells. top with whipped cream and garnish with slices of lemon peel.

Mousse Pie
Spoon filling into a prepared graham cracker crust and freeze overnight. Remove from freezer and top with meringue.
Bake 400°F (200°C) 4-6 minutes. Return to freezer until serving time. Enough filling for 2 pies.

Jiffy Cake

Variations on a theme.

3	Tbsp	soft butter	45 mL
1		egg	1
½	cup	milk	125 mL
1	cup	sugar	250 mL
		grated rind of 1 orange	
1½	cups	cake flour	375 mL
1½	tsp	baking powder	7 mL
¼	tsp	salt	2 mL

Preheat oven to 350°F (180°C). Mix first 4 ingredients in bowl. Sift dry ingredients and add. Beat together until smooth. Pour into 8x8" (19x19cm) cake pan and bake for 35 minutes.
While cake is still warm, perforate with a tooth pick and pour over sauce made of ⅓ cup (75mL) sugar and juice of 1 orange.

Variations:
1. Substitute 1 tsp (5mL) vanilla for orange rind; ice with vanilla frosting and decorate with cherries, nuts, or chocolate chips.
2. Substitute ¼ cup (50mL) cocoa for ¼ cup (50mL) flour; frost with chocolate icing.
3. Make upside down cake by lining pan with any fruit, e.g. apple slices coated with brown sugar and melted butter. Serve with a hot lemon sauce.
Serves 8.

Quick Cheesecake

A lot of effect with little effort!

1		graham cracker pie shell	1
1	cup	icing sugar	250 mL
1		pkg (8oz/227mL) cream cheese	1
1		pkg Dream whip	1
		fresh fruit or 1 can (19oz/540mL) cherry pie filling	
½	tsp	almond flavouring	2 mL

Beat together sugar and cheese. Prepare Dream whip and add to cheese mixture. Pour into crust. Refrigerate. Before serving, top with fresh fruit or pie filling mixed with almond flavouring.
Serves 8.

Peanut Brittle Dessert

The "I hate to make dessert" dessert!

2	cups	whipping cream	500 mL
1	cup	brown sugar	250 mL
10	oz	peanut brittle	300 g
1		large angel food cake	1

Put cream and sugar in a large bowl; leave overnight (or all day), stirring occasionally to blend well. Crumble peanut brittle (or use the food processor). Whip cream mixture until it forms peaks; add about ⅓ peanut brittle. Cut cake in 3 layers; ice each layer and the top with cream, adding more peanut brittle (will probably not use all). Let stand in refrigerator about 2 hours. Light and delicious!
Serves 8-10

Mum's Nut Torte

3		egg whites	3
¼	tsp	cream of tartar	1 mL
1	cup	sugar	250 mL
1	tsp	vanilla	5 mL
¾	cup	chopped walnuts or filberts	175 mL
20		ritz crackers, crushed	20
2	cups	cream, whipped	500 mL
		chocolate shavings, nuts, or cherries	

Preheat oven to 325°F (160°C). Beat egg whites until stiff. Beat in next 3 ingredients. Fold in nuts and crackers. Spoon into 2 greased round pans approximately 8″ (20cm) in diameter.
Bake for 30 minutes. Cool for 15 minutes and remove from pans. Layer cake, cream, cake, cream. Decorate with chocolate, nuts, or cherries. Let stand for 12 hours in refrigerator.
Serves 8.

Pears Baked in Raspberry Sauce

A colorful ending to an elegant dinner.

6		firm ripe pears, peeled	6	
1½	cups	water	375	mL
1	cup	sugar	250	mL
1		pkg (15oz/450g) frozen raspberries	1	
2	tsp	cornstarch	10	mL
3	Tbsp	fruit liqueur	45	mL
1	tsp	vanilla	5	mL
		whipped cream		

Combine water, sugar and berries in a heavy saucepan. Poach pears gently in syrup until tender 15 - 20 minutes. Remove. Strain syrup and return to pan. Dissolve cornstarch in a small amount of cold water. Stir into syrup and cook and stir until slightly thickened. Stir in liqueur and vanilla. Pour over pears and chill until serving time. Serve in stemmed glass dishes decorated with whipped cream.
Note: Trim the bottom of the pears so they will sit flat in the dishes.
Serves 6.

Blueberry Sauce for Crepes

1		pkg (10oz/284g) frozen blueberries	1	
½	cup	sugar	125	mL
1	Tbsp	cornstarch	15	mL
¼	tsp	nutmeg	1	mL
1	Tbsp	lemon juice	15	mL
1		banana, sliced	1	

Thaw berries. Combine all ingredients, except bananas, in a heavy saucepan. Cook over medium heat stirring constantly until thickened. Add sliced banana. Cool 5-10 minutes. Fill crepes with vanilla ice cream, roll up, spoon sauce over.
Note: Also good over ice cream.
Enough sauce for 6 - 8 crepes.

Barb's Topping

Use as an icing and filling for cakes.

⅓	cup	sugar	75 mL
2	Tbsp	instant coffee	30 mL
⅛	tsp	salt	.5 mL
2	cups	whipping cream	500 mL

Chill ingredients and then beat until stiff.
Makes about 4 cups (1L) topping.

Fruit Frosting or Filling

Spoon over angel food, sponge or banana cakes.

1	cup	fruit, strawberry, raspberry or banana	250 mL
1	cup	sugar	250 mL
1		egg white	1

If fruit has been frozen, drain off some of the liquid. Beat ingredients together at high speed on electric mixer until stiff. This is best made just before serving so egg white does not separate.
Makes 2 cups (500mL) filling.

Cookies & Squares

Chocolate Cheesecake Brownies

Two additions to a brownie lover's repertoire.

Chocolate Layer

½	lb	soft butter	250	g
2	cups	sugar	500	mL
4		eggs	4	
½	tsp	salt	2	mL
1	cup	cocoa	250	mL
1	cup	flour	250	mL
1	cup	chopped walnuts or pecans	250	mL

Cheesecake Layer

1	cup	sugar	250	mL
2		pkgs (8oz/250g) cream cheese, softened	2	
2		eggs	2	
1½	tsp	vanilla	7	mL

Preheat oven to 350°F (180°C).

For chocolate layer cream butter and sugar. Add eggs one at a time beating well after each addition. Mix in salt, cocoa and flour and stir in nuts. Set aside.

For cheesecake layer combine ingredients and beat until smooth. In a greased 9x13" (3L) cake pan, spread a little less than half the chocolate batter. Spread cheesecake layer over. Add the remaining chocolate in small dabs over the top. It won't spread and there may be bits of white showing. Not to worry as chocolate will spread somewhat while baking. Bake 30 minutes.
Frost with your favorite chocolate icing if desired, but not necessary. Makes about 36 squares.

Chocolate Dreams

Like a very fudgie brownie. Easy to make and yummy!

1	cup	margarine	250	mL
4		squares unsweetened chocolate	4	
2	cups	sugar	500	mL
4		eggs well beaten	4	
1	tsp	vanilla	5	mL
1¼	cups	flour	300	mL
½	tsp	salt	2	mL
1	cup	chopped walnuts	250	mL

Frosting

2		squares unsweetened chocolate	2	
3	Tbsp	hot water	45	mL
1	Tbsp	butter	15	mL
2	cups	icing sugar	500	mL
1	tsp	vanilla	5	mL
1		egg	1	

Preheat oven to 400°F (200°C). Melt shortening and chocolate in a mixing bowl over hot water. Add sugar mixing to dissolve sugar. Add eggs and vanilla. Mix well. Add flour and salt. Mix again. Remove from heat and stir in nuts. Spread in a 9x13" (3.5L) greased cakepan. Bake 18 minutes. Cool and ice.

Frosting
Melt chocolate with water over hot water. Blend in butter. Cool. Add sugar, vanilla and beat in egg. Mixture will be very runny - like a glaze. Spread over the chocolate dreams and cut when cool.
Makes 36 squares.

Deluxe Pecan Squares

Oh so decadent! Pecan pie in a square.

Base
1	cup	butter	250 mL
⅓	cup	brown sugar	75 mL
1		egg	1
1	tsp	lemon juice	5 mL
3	cups	flour	750 mL
3	cups	whole pecans	750 mL

Topping
1	cup	butter	250 mL
9	Tbsp	honey	135 mL
1	cup	brown sugar	250 mL
3	Tbsp	whipping cream	45 mL

Preheat oven to 350°F (180°C). For the base combine the first 5 ingredients. Press into a buttered 9x13" (3.5L) cake pan. Prick with a fork.
Bake 20 minutes. Spread pecans over base.
In a heavy saucepan cook together the next 3 ingredients until brown (5 minutes) whisking constantly. Add whipping cream and stir. Spread over the pecans.
Bake 20 minutes. Cut into small squares.
Makes 36 squares.

O'Henry Bars

⅔	cup	melted butter or margarine	150 mL
1	cup	brown sugar	250 mL
4	cups	rolled oats	1 L
½	cup	corn syrup	125 mL
1	Tbsp	vanilla	15 mL
		pinch salt	

Topping

1	cup	chocolate chips	250 mL
⅔	cup	crunchy peanut butter	150 mL

Preheat oven to 375°F (190°C). Mix the first 6 ingredients until well blended. Press into a 9x13" (22x34cm) buttered pan.
Bake for 15 minutes.
Cool slightly. Melt chocolate chips and peanut butter in double boiler. Spread over base.
Makes 36 squares.

Welsh Cakes

2	cups	flour	500 mL
1	tsp	baking powder	5 mL
½	tsp	nutmeg	2 mL
⅛	tsp	salt	.5 mL
1	cup	shortening, ½ butter and ½ margarine	250 mL
½	cup	sugar	125 mL
1		egg, well beaten	1
¾	cup	currants	175 mL

Stir together the first 4 ingredients. Cream together the next 2 ingredients. Add egg and blend. Add dry ingredients and currants, mixing to form a stiff dough. Turn out onto a lightly floured surface and roll ⅜" (1cm) thick. Cut in small rounds and place in greased frying pan over medium heat. Cook 4 minutes on each side, being careful not to burn.
Makes 8 dozen.

Jumbo Chewy Oatmeal Cookies

Jumbo cookies are fun for a change!

1	cup	butter	250 mL
¾	cup	sugar	175 mL
¾	cup	brown sugar	175 mL
1		egg	1
1	tsp	vanilla	5 mL
1	cup	flour	250 mL
½	tsp	baking soda	2 mL
1-2	tsp	cinnamon	5-10 mL
2½	cups	oats (not instant)	625 mL
½	cup	coconut (optional)	125 mL
1¼	cups	raisins	300 mL

Preheat oven to 350°F (180°C). Cream first 5 ingredients, beating well. Stir together next 6 ingredients and add to batter. Drop by heaping Tbsp on greased cookie sheets. Space well apart - at least 3" (8cm). Pat each cookie lightly with finger just to neaten up.
Bake for 11-12 minutes. Do not overbake, or cookies will not be chewy. Cool on racks.
Note: For Chunky Chocolate Oatmeal Cookies, substitute a large bar of semi-sweet chocolate (in pieces) for the raisins and reduce cinnamon to 1 tsp (5mL).
Makes 26-30 large cookies.

Nancy's Oatmeal Pecan Cookies

1	cup	butter	250 mL
1	tsp	baking soda	5 mL
½	tsp	salt	2 mL
½	tsp	cinnamon	2 mL
1		egg	1
1	tsp	vanilla	5 mL
1	cup	white sugar	250 mL
½	cup	brown sugar	125 mL
2	cups	flour	500 mL
1½	cups	large flake oats	375 mL
1	cup	coconut or very finely chopped pecans	250 mL
		pecan halves	

Preheat oven to 350°F (180°C). In the large bowl of electric mixer beat the first 4 ingredients. Add the next 4 and beat well. Blend in the next 3 ingredients. On a greased cookie sheet make large drop cookies, flatten with fork and press a pecan half into the centre of each.
Bake for 14-16 minutes.
Makes 36 cookies.

Shortbread

1	cup	sugar	250 mL
1	cup	butter	250 mL
1		egg yolk	1
2½	cups	flour	625 mL
½	cup	finely chopped walnuts	125 mL

Preheat oven to 325°F (160°C). Cream butter and sugar. Add beaten yolk. Add flour and nuts. Mix well. Form into 1 or 2 rolls. Refrigerate 2 hours or more (will keep a few days). Slice dough and place on cookie sheet.
Bake until slightly brown.
Makes 24 cookies.

Granny's Apricot Squares

These are even better if allowed to mellow for a couple of days.

⅔	cup	diced dried apricots	150 mL
⅔	cup	water	150 mL
½	cup	butter	125 mL
¼	cup	sugar	50 mL
1	cup	sifted flour	250 mL
½	cup	flour	125 mL
½	tsp	baking powder	2 mL
¼	tsp	salt	1 mL
2		eggs, well beaten	2
¾	cup	brown sugar	175 mL
1	tsp	vanilla	5 mL
½	cup	coconut or chopped nuts	125 mL

Preheat oven to 350°F (180°C). Simmer apricots in water for 15 minutes. Cool. Mix butter, sugar and 1 cup flour until crumbly. Press into a greased 7x13" (17x34cm) cake pan.
Bake for 20 minutes.
Sift flour, baking powder and salt. Beat together the next three ingredients. Stir in flour mixture. Add fruit and nuts and mix thoroughly. Pour over baked crust.
Bake 30 minutes more. Cool in pan. Frost with a thin lemon icing. Makes 30 bars.

Dolly Bars

½	cup	butter	125 mL
¼	cup	icing sugar	50 mL
1	tsp	cinnamon	5 mL
2	cups	graham cracker crumbs	500 mL
1	cup	chocolate chips	250 mL
1	cup	walnuts	250 mL
1	cup	coconut	250 mL
1		can (14oz/398mL) Eagle Brand sweetened condensed milk	1

Preheat oven to 350°F (180°C). Melt butter in 9x13" (23x30cm) baking dish while mixing the next 3 ingredients. Sprinkle crumb mixture over melted butter; pat down to make crust. Sprinkle next 3 ingredients over crust and pour milk over all.
Bake 30 minutes. Cut into squares while still warm.
Makes 36 squares.

K.C.J. Bars

A quick change from Nanaimo bars but just as rich! "Easy for kids to make," say Kim, Chris and Jamie.

1½	cups	graham wafer crumbs	375 mL
½	cup	butter, melted	125 mL
1		sweetened, long thread coconut can sweetened condensed milk	1
12	oz	chocolate chips, melted	350 g
¾	cup	crunchy peanut butter	175 mL

Preheat oven to 350°F (180°C). Combine crumbs and butter. Pack well into a buttered 8" (20cm) square pan and bake for 20 minutes. Sprinkle a layer of coconut over base, barely covering it. Pour sweetened condensed milk evenly over coconut. Bake 20 minutes longer - until it looks almost set. Melt chocolate chips and peanut butter over hot (not boiling) water, and pour over cooked bars.
Makes 25 squares.

Jessie's Cherry Squares

½	cup	butter	125 mL
1	cup	flour	250 mL
2	Tbsp	icing sugar	30 mL
1	cup	white sugar	250 mL
2	Tbsp	butter	30 mL
2		eggs	2
1	tsp	almond extract	5 mL
½	cup	chopped walnuts	125 mL
½	cup	mixed candied fruit	125 mL
1	cup	sliced candied or maraschino cherries	250 mL
¾	cup	flour	175 mL
1	tsp	baking powder	5 mL

Icing

2	Tbsp	butter	30 mL
1	cup	sifted icing sugar	250 mL
¼	cup	cherry juice	50 mL
⅛	tsp	almond extract	.5 mL

Preheat oven to 325°F (160°C). Mix together the first 3 ingredients and press into an 8" (20cm) square pan.
Bake 20 minutes. Cool. Beat together the next 4 ingredients, add remaining ingredients mixing thoroughly. Spread batter over cooled base. Increase oven to 350°F (180°C) and bake 30 minutes. Combine ingredients for icing and beat until smooth. Spread over cooled squares. Makes 25 squares.

Wellington Squares

Base

½	cup	butter	125	mL
¼	cup	sugar	50	mL
1		egg	1	
½	tsp	vanilla	2	mL
1¼	cups	flour	300	mL

Filling

1	cup	butter	250	mL
⅓	cup	white sugar	75	mL
¼	cup	corn syrup	50	mL
1		can sweetened condensed milk	1	
½	tsp	vanilla	2	mL

Topping

6	oz	chocolate chips	180	g

Preheat oven to 350°F (180°C).

Base
Cream butter, sugar, egg and vanilla. Add flour, making a stiff dough. Press into a 9x13" (3.5L) greased cake pan and bake 20 minutes or until brown. It will shrink slightly. Cool completely.

Filling
Mix ingredients together in a heavy saucepan over low heat. Bring to a boil, stirring constantly and boil 10 minutes. Remove from heat and add vanilla. Pour over cooled base. Cool completely. Melt chocolate chips and spread over filling. Cut into squares when chocolate is firm, but not hard. This freezes well.
Makes 36 squares.

Mom's Super Butter Tarts

¾	cup	brown sugar	175	mL
¼	cup	soft butter	50	mL
1		egg	1	
1	tsp	vanilla	5	mL
½	cup	chopped dates	125	mL
⅓	cup	chopped walnuts	75	mL
12		unbaked tart shells	12	

Preheat oven to 450°F (230°C). Mix first 4 ingredients just until blended. Add next 2 ingredients and divide mixture among tart shells. Bake for 10 minutes. Do not overbake or the centres will not be syrupy. Filling for 12 medium tart shells.

Peanut Butter Delights

1	cup	peanut butter	250	mL
1	Tbsp	softened butter	15	mL
1	cup	icing sugar	250	mL
1	cup	chopped nuts	250	mL
1	cup	mixed diced fruit or rice krispies	250	mL
		plain butter icing		
		crushed nuts or fine coconut		

Cream together the first 3 ingredients. Add nuts and fruit. Mold into little balls. Coat with butter icing and roll in crushed nuts or fine coconut. Keep refrigerated.
Makes 48 small balls.

Et Cetera

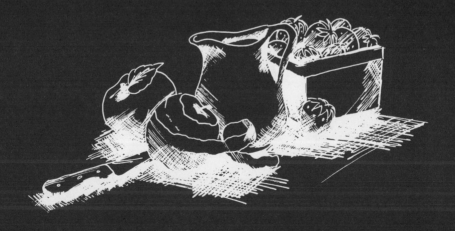

Fluffy Mustard Sauce for Ham

Good with other meats too!

2		beaten egg yolks	2
1	Tbsp	sugar	15 mL
3	Tbsp	prepared mustard	45 mL
2	Tbsp	vinegar	30 mL
1	Tbsp	water	15 mL
½	tsp	salt	2 mL
1	Tbsp	butter or margarine	15 mL
1	Tbsp	prepared horseradish	15 mL
½	cup	whipping cream, whipped	125 mL

To egg yolks, stir in the next 5 ingredients. Cook over hot, not boiling, water until thickened, about 5 minutes. Remove from heat; blend in butter and horseradish; cool completely. Fold in whipped cream. Store in fridge; serve at room temperature.
Makes 1½ cups(325mL).

Uncooked Indian Relish

Great on a hotdog, with pork or practically anything.

18		ripe tomatoes	18
7		large onions	7
1		large bunch celery	1
½	cup	salt	125 mL
2		sweet green peppers chopped	2
2		sweet red peppers chopped	2
2	cups	white vinegar	500 mL
1	oz	white mustard seed	30 g
6	cups	sugar	1.5 L

Chop first 3 ingredients and cover with salt. Let stand overnight; drain. Add remaining ingredients, stir without crushing. Let stand 1 day, stirring occasionally. Bottle and wax.
Makes about 6 pints(3L).

Aunt Shirley's Salmon Sauce

1		pkg Lawrey's Lemon Garlic Salad Dressing Mix	1
2½	cups	mayonnaise	625 mL
3	Tbsp	lemon juice	45 mL
		dill to taste	

Mix all ingredients except dill. Spread on salmon - sprinkle with dill and bake.
Enough sauce for 1 very large salmon.

Fish Sauce

2	tsp	soy sauce	10 mL
⅓	cup	sherry	75 mL
¾	cup	butter, melted and cooled	175 mL
2		garlic cloves	2
2	tsp	dry mustard	10 mL
3	Tbsp	ketchup	45 mL

Mix all ingredients, and serve with plain fish entree.

Crème Fraîche

Make at least 12 hours before using.

2	cups	heavy cream	500 mL
2	tsp	buttermilk	10 mL

Pour cream into jar, add buttermilk and stir. Cover tightly and let stand in slightly warm place for 12 hours or more.
Makes 2 cups(500mL).

Lemon Cheese

½	cup	butter	125 mL
2	cups	sugar	500 mL
6		large eggs, beaten	6
		rind and juice of 3 lemons	
		or	
⅓	cup	bottled lemon juice	75 mL

Combine all ingredients in saucepan. Stir until smooth. Simmer until thick. Store in airtight jars in refrigerator. Good as a filling for tart shells or as a spread.

Iced Almonds

1½	cups	whole blanched almonds	375 mL
½	cup	sugar	125 mL
2	Tbsp	butter	30 mL

Heat ingredients in a heavy skillet over medium heat stirring constantly until almonds are toasted and sugar is golden and syrupy, about 10 minutes. Drop nuts onto a sheet of aluminum foil. Cool.

Rhubarb Conserve

1		whole orange, cut in chunks	1
1		whole lemon, cut in chunks	1
3	cups	sliced rhubarb	750 mL
1		large pineapple, pared, cored and chopped	1
¼	lb	almonds	125 g
5	cups	sugar	1250 mL

Place orange and lemon chunks in a blender and process until coarsely chopped. Add to a large heavy saucepan along with the remaining ingredients. Simmer gently for one hour or until thick. Pour into container.

Index

Almonds, iced	176
Almond tarte	152
Angle mousse	147
Apple cheesecake tarte	140
Antipasto	3
Apricot bread	125
Apricot squares, granny's	168
Artichoke hearts, hot	4
Avocado, special	25
Bananas, baked	150
Bananas, B.J.'s	145
Banana chocolate chip muffins	131
Barley with mushrooms	102
Bean casserole, green	88
Beans Viennese style, green	89

Beef:
Cheese and meat casserole	112
Chinese sweet 'n sour meatballs	16
Crescent Italiano bake	114
Greek meatloaf	76
Liver and bacon	119
Meatballs	120
Meat loaf	107
Minute meat loaf	107
Peppered roast beef	72
Pot roast with noodles	111
Shepherd's pie plus	106
Sweet and Sauer burger	119

Beef and horseradish salad	48
Blueberry Kuchen	146
Blueberry sauce for crêpes	159
Blueberry yogurt muffins	132
Blue cheese dressing	57
Bongo Bongo soup	30
Boston clam chowder	33

Breads:
Apricot	125
Easy cheese	128
English muffins in a loaf	126
French onion	127
Mexican corn	129
Mozzarella	127
Onion sour cream	127
Pumpkin loaf	124
Take one French loaf	127
Tasty fruit loaf	125
Toasted herb rolls in a loaf	128
Wheaten	138

Broccoli casserole	88
Broccoli soup, cream of	36
Broccoli and carrot timbale	97
Brochette of pork	74
Brownies, chocolate cheesecake	162
Brussel sprouts, bon vivant	91
Burger, sweet 'n sauer	119
Butter tarts, mom's	172
Cabbage, scalloped	93
Cabbage soup, Irv's mother's	38

Cakes:
Barb's topping	160
Fruit frosting	160
Jiffy cake	156
Gâteau au Rhum	143
Peanut Brittle Dessert	157

Carrot pineapple muffins, special	130
Carrot curry soup	39
Carrots, 40 carat	94

Casseroles:
Cheese and meat	112
Cheesy spinach lasagne	116
Church supper tuna bake	109
Eggs royale	104
Paella à la Valencianna	70
Shrimp	110
Shrimp green noodle	67

Cauliflower, frosted	101
Caviar, fake	104
Caviar pie	19
Cheese ball, dessert	147
Cheese, fried, Italian style	18
Cheese bread, easy	128
Cherry squares, Jessie's	170

Chicken:
Dijon	81
"McNug's"	115
Parmegiana	80
Parmesan	115
Royale	69
Wings	12,13
With herbed carrot sauce	79
Chow Mein	108
Honey Lemon	78
Orange	78

Chocolate cheesecake brownies	162
Chocolate cheesecake	151
Chocolate coffee cake	135
Chocolate dreams	163
Chocolate mint pie, decadent	150
Chocolate rum pie	142
Chocolate mocha pie	154
Chops, pork barbeque	118
Chops, veal à la Wendy	71
Clam chowder, Boston	33
Clam chowder, Manhattan	32
Clam puffs	10

Coffee cakes:
Chocolate	135
Cranberry	137
Fresh fruit	134
Marble	138
Poppy seed	136

Consommé, California	43

Cookies:
    Jumbo chewy oatmeal 166
    Nancy's oatmeal pecan 167
    Oatmeal shortbread 168
    Peanut butter delights 172
    Shortbread 167
    Welsh cakes 165
Cornbread, Mexican 129
Corn custard, baked 99
Crab:
    Bisque 43
    Crèpes gratin 62
    Crab supper pie 113
    Cream cheese & crab delight 2
    Howe sound crab mousse 7
    Nuts over crab 46
Cranberry coffee cake 137
Crème fraîche 175
Creole, shrimp 66
Crèpes, crab gratin 62
Crescent Italiano bake 114
Curried seafood, quick 63
Desserts:
    Almond tarte 152
    Angel mousse 147
    Apple cheesecake tarte 140
    Baked bananas 150
    B.J.'s bananas 145
    Blueberry kuchen 146
    Chocolate cheesecake 151
    Chocolate mocha pie 154
    Chocolate rum pie 142
    Decadent chocolate mint pie 150
    Dessert cheese ball 147
    Fresh fruit tarte 144
    Fruit kabobs 141
    Gâteau au rhum 143
    German cheese cake with tart cherries ... 149
    Jiffy cake 156
    Mix 'n match frozen lemon mousse 155
Dolly bars 169
Dressings:
    Blue cheese 57
    Cora's Caesar 57
    Chutney 51
    Mary's French 56
    Peanut sauce 52
    Soy sauce vinaigrette 56
    Yogurt 58
Eggs royale casserole 104
Emerald salad 49
English muffins in a loaf 126
Fish
    Red snapper and crab in wine sauce 83
    Trout Meunière 82
Fish sauce 175
Fraudulent frill 43
French dressing, Mary's 56

French onion bread 127
Fresh fruit coffee cake 134
Fresh fruit tarte 144
Fruit frosting or filling 160
Fruit kabobs 141
Fruit loaf, tasty 125
Fruit pudding, rategrutze 141
Fusilli shrimp salad, Mark's 24
Gâteau au rhum 143
Gouda squares 10
Goulash soup 37
Gravlax, Mary's 11
Ham and cheese soup 41
Ham in croûte 68
Hamburger soup, hearty 40
Herb rolls in a loaf, toasted 128
Indonesian salad 52
K.C.J. Bars 169
Krabbenauflauf with cheese 105
Kuchen, blueberry 146
Lamb, Henri's leg of 77
Lasagne, cheesy spinach 116
Leek and stilton soup 43
Lemon cheese 176
Lemon mousse, mix 'n match frozen 155
Liver and bacon 119
Manhattan clam chowder 32
Marble coffee cake 138
Marinated pork roast 75
Meatballs 120
Meat & cheese casserole 112
Meatloaf:
    Meatloaf 107
    Greek 76
    Minute 107
Mexican flour tortilla rolls 14
Mozzarella bread 127
Muffins:
    Banana chocolate chip 131
    Blueberry Yogurt 132
    Special pineapple carrot 130
    Sunshine orange 133
    Wheatgerm 133
Mustard sauce 11
Mustard sauce for ham, fluffy 174
Mystery salad 46
Nasi Goreng 122
Nut torte, mum's 158
Oatmeal cookies, jumbo chewy 166
Oatmeal pecan cookies, Nancy's 167
Oatmeal shortbread 168
O'Henry bars 165
Onion rounds 8
Onion shortcake 95
Onion sour cream bread 127
Orange muffins, sunshine 133
Paella à la Valencianna 70

Pasta Sauces:
   Fetta mata shrimp sauce 27
   Pasta alle vongole 26
   Pasta pronto 26
   Pesto pasta 27
   Scallops Provençale and avocado 28
Paté mock aspic 4
Paw paw au gratin 98
Peanut sauce 52
Peanut brittle dessert 157
Peanut butter delight 172
Pears baked in raspberry sauce 159
Peas, oriental 93
Pecan squares, deluxe 164
Peppered roast beef 72
Pilaf, sesame 102
Poppy seed coffee cake 136
Pork:
   Barbeque pork chops 118
   Brochette of 74
   Ham en croûte 68
   Marinated pork roast 75
   Perennial boar 60
   South seas 64
   Spareribs 118
   Tourtière 121
Pot roast with noodles 111
Potato casserole, big 92
Potato salad, Mme Benoit's 50
Potato soup, scalloped 31
Potato tomato bake 100
Prunes, Alice B. Toklas 145
Pumpkin loaf 124
Quiche:
   Quiche me quick 60
   Crab supper pie 113
Raspberry ribbon pie 148
Rategrutze 141
Red snapper and crab in wine sauce 83
Relish, uncooked Indian 174
Rhubarb conserve 176
Rhubarb pie 153
Rice salad, two 47
Salads:
   Beef and Horseradish 48
   Buffet shrimp and avocado 49
   Emerald 49
   Indonesian 52
   Jellied shrimp 50
   Marinated zucchini 54
   Mme Benoit's potato 50
   Mystery 46
   Nuts over crab 46
   À la cité 53
   Spinach salad with a difference 51
   Taco 61
   Two rice 47
   Zucchini tabbouleh 55

Sauces:
   Aunt Shirley's Salmon 175
   Blueberry 159
   Fish 175
   Fluffy mustard for ham 174
   Mustard 11
   Plum 15
   Vegetable 101
Scallops:
   Gratin de coquille St. Jacques 22
   Scallops in crème fraîche sauce........... 85
Seafood, curried quick 63
Seafood salad bowls 21

Shepherd's pie plus 106
Shortbread 167
Shrimp:
   Buffet shrimp and avocado 49
   Shrimp casserole 110
   Creole 66
   Shrimp green noodle casserole 67
   Jellied shrimp salad 50
   Krabbenauflauf with cheese 105
   Sweet 'n sour 65
Sole:
   Au vin blanc 117
   Florentine 84
   Fourées 86
   Terrine of sole and salmon 20
Soups:
   Bongo bongo soup 30
   Boston clam showder 33
   California consommé 43
   Carrot curry soup 39
   Crab bisque 43
   Cream of broccoli soup 36
   Creamy tomato 42
   Goulash 37
   Ham and cheese 41
   Hearty hamburger 40
   Irv's mother's cabbage 38
   Leek and stilton 43
   Manhattan clam chowder 32
   Pacific salmon chowder 34
   Scalloped potato 31
   Spring tonic 44
   Zucchini 35
Soy sauce vinegrette 56
Spare ribs 118
Spinach rolls, Greek 5
Squash casserole, delicious 89
Squares:
   Chocolate cheesecake brownies 162
   Chocolate dreams 163
   Dolly bars 169
   Granny's apricot 168
   Jessie's cherry 170
   K.C.J. bars 169

O'Henry bars 165
Pecan deluxe 164
Wellington Squares 171
Starters:
   Caviar pie 19
   Fried cheese Italian style 18
   Gratin de coquille St. Jacques 22
   Mark's fusili shrimp salad 24
   Salmon tartare with black caviar 23
   Seafood salad bowls 21
   Smoked salmon mousse 19
   Special avocado 25
   Terrine of sole and salmon 20
Sweet and Sauer burger 119
Sweet 'n sour shrimp 65
Taco salad 61
Tomatoes with pine nuts 96
Tomato soup, creamy 42
Torte, mom's nut 158
Tourtière 121
Trout Meunière 82
Tuna:
   Church supper tuna bake 109
   In shells 117
   Teasers 9
Veal:
   Veal chops a la Wendy 71
   Veal scallops in creamy sauce 72
   Vitello Tonnato 73
Vegetables:
   Baked corn custard 99
   Barley with mushrooms 102
   Big potato casserole 92
   Broccoli casserole 88
   Brussel sprouts bon vivant 91
   40 Carat carrots 94
   Carrot and broccoli timbale 97
   Delicious squash casserole 89
   Frosted Cauliflower 101
   Green bean casserole 88
   Green beans, Viennese style 89
   Onion shortcake 95
   Oriental peas 93
   Paw paw au gratin 98
   Potato tomato bake 100
   Scalloped cabbage 93
   Sesame pilaf 102
   Tomatoes with pine nuts 96
   Zucchini casserole 90
   Zucchini Italiana 90
Vitello Tonnato 73
Welsh cakes 165
Wheat germ muffins 133
Wheaten bread 138
Yogurt dressings 58
Zucchini casserole 90
Zucchini Italiana 90

Zucchini salad, marinated 54
Zucchini soup 35
Zucchini tabbouleh 55